SHAYNDL
and
SALOMEA
From Lemberg to Berlin

SALOMEA GENIN

Translated by Brigitte Goldstein
With an Afterword by Wolfgang Benz

NORTHWESTERN UNIVERSITY PRESS

Evanston, Illinois

Northwestern University Press
Evanston, Illinois 60208-4210

Originally published in German under the title *Scheindl und Salomea: Von Lemberg nach Berlin*. Copyright © 1992 by Fischer Taschenbuch Verlag, GmbH, Frankfurt am Main. English translation copyright © 1997 by Brigitte Goldstein. Published 1997 by Northwestern University Press. All rights reserved.

Printed in the United States of America

ISBN 0-8101-1183-7 (cloth)
ISBN 0-8101-1168-3 (paper)

Library of Congress Cataloging-in-Publication Data

Genin, Salomea, 1932–
    [Scheindl und Salomea. English]
    Shayndl and Salomea / Salomea Genin ; translated by
Brigitte Goldstein ; with an afterword by Wolfgang Benz.
    p. cm.
    ISBN 0-8101-1183-7 (cloth). — ISBN 0-8101-1168-3 (paper)
    1. Genin, Salomea, 1932– . 2. Jews, East European—
Germany—Berlin—Biography. 3. Jewish children—Germany—Berlin—
Biography. 4. Berlin (Germany)—Biography. I. Title.
DS135.G5G432413 1997
940.53'18'092243155—dc21
[B]   97-2492
                                            CIP
                                            r97

Shayndl and Salomea

Dedicated to my two sisters

One has never seen that unfree people love one another. They may come together to do good or bad, but they cannot love.

THEODOR LESSING

Without love we are mortal, immortal when we love.

KARL JASPERS

✻

Contents

❖

Acknowledgments

My thanks go to Jan Bereska, who broke down my resistance to looking at my grandfather and what he really meant to me; to Christa Tragelehn, who urged me to write; to Karsten Troyke, for his sensitive and understanding editing; to my psychotherapist, without whom this story would never have been written in this way; to the many friends who read the original German manuscript and encouraged me to continue; and, last but not least, to Brigitte Goldstein, who translated it into English and in course became a friend.

Shayndl and Salomea

✿

I Don't Remember

. . . my deeply religious grandfather, because he died in Lemberg (Lvov) in 1930, where he lived and for decades published books in Hebrew and Yiddish.

. . . the radiant beauty and romantic naïveté of my mother—the sixth child and second daughter—while she was growing up in a crowded apartment at 9 Rzeznicka Street in Lemberg's Jewish quarter, because she was already thirty-six years old in 1932 when I was born.

. . . her relationship with her parents, her seven brothers, and one sister, who deeply influenced my mother, because I have a clear recollection of only two of my uncles.

. . . the trauma my mother suffered because her father sat shiva (the Jewish rite of mourning for the dead) for her, although she was quite alive—a practice or malpractice in Jewish families when their children go too far in breaking the accepted norms—because she insisted on marrying my father.

I don't remember, and yet it all lived concealed within me. I often awoke at night with the feeling that my bed was a coffin and that I did not deserve to be alive. Thus, I was unable to just live; instead I needed a justification for living, a purpose in life, which I found in the fight for a just society.

I repudiated God and Torah. Yet, imbued as I was with a profound religiosity, I made the teachings of socialism my religion, the Communist Party my church, and its ideologues my prophets. Endowed with my mother's romantic naïveté, I believed I could help realize an idyllic society. With the glowing fervor and devotion that was my grandfather's, I embraced the cause of a better world for all human beings. Like both of them, I lived in constant expectation of the next pogrom and was convinced that I could only escape it by fleeing.

Existential fear gripped me whenever I fell in love, a fear I experienced as abuse from my lover. I raged against this "abuse" until the relationship was destroyed and I could sink back, relieved, into my loneliness.

At the age of fifty, I lost all will to live. I sought and found help. I began to write. From stories told and untold, from fragments known, sensed, and imagined, I tried to create a picture of the world that had formed my mother.

In March 1988, I thought I had completed this book. One reader said: "Your relatives from Lemberg have no flesh and blood. They act like wooden puppets. Try again." Only then did I become aware of the psychic barrier that separated me from the world of my grandparents, a barrier I had carried within me all my life. When I tried to break through it, I fell into a paralyzing abyss. A voice within me warned: You must not write this, you must not write this! Suddenly I knew that my grandfather's declaring my mother dead—which I heard about for the first time at age fifty—was the skeleton I had to drag from the family closet. Only then would I be able to halt the decay that had eaten at my soul all my life. I also knew that the voice of warning was that of my mother's father. I shouted back at him: "You not only did this terrible thing to my mother, you are also too cowardly to admit it. And I've been burdened with it all my life! Enough!"

For four months I wrote defiantly, spelling out his guilt. I believed I could outwit him. When I had finished, I realized that I had also outwitted myself. By reviving his world on paper, I got to know him; I got to know his uprightness and his strict adherence to principles, his kindness and his vulnerability, and also his dedication to the common good. Thus he was able to forgive himself— and I, too, was able to forgive him—for the pain and the damage he had caused the one he loved most: my mother—and, through her, me. When I had finished writing a second time, he was no longer my mother's father, but my Opa Shulim.

❀

Shulim—1910

Shulim Zwerling was not a very tall man. He had a graying beard that had never been touched by a pair of scissors. Every morning before breakfast he hurried out of the house to say his morning prayers in shul, in the synagogue. There he felt closer to God, whose holy name no one is permitted to utter. The service begins when ten men are assembled in a minyan—God forbid there should be only nine. Shulim would never miss a service without a good reason.

It was still dark when he crossed Legionov Boulevard at seven o'clock; he passed the opera house, and, looking right and left, he safely reached the other side of the expansive roadway. He walked up the steps of the imposing synagogue, through the foyer, and entered a large, dimly lit hall. Up front near the pulpit, the light of several burning candles illuminated the two tablets of the Ten Commandments on the wall and the stained-glass windows in which a Mogen Duvid, a Star of David, gleamed dark blue.

More than a thousand people crowded the shul on the High Holidays. The women were separated from the men and sat in the gallery on the second floor. But on this day there were only a handful of men in the front rows. Shulim took the seat that bore his name and looked around, greeting everyone with a barely perceptible nod of the head. Almost thirty. Good enough, he thought. He knew that early in the morning there would not be much talking. The men were preoccupied with themselves, seeking contemplation before setting out for the day's work. Here was the community he needed; this was his second family. It was the source of his inner strength, of his inner peace. All commonplace concerns vanished in communal prayer.

The cantor at the pulpit lifted his clear tenor voice, chanting the Hebrew words of the daily prayers. Some of the men followed along in the prayer book, mumbling softly; others, like Shulim, closed their eyes and, swaying back and forth, chanted along in a clearly audible singsong. For a stranger, the entire scene may seem incomprehensible, sounding like quickly rattled off babbling and mumbling to the tune of an exotic melody. For Shulim prayer was the pillar and center of his existence. Soft and loud, chanting and mumbling, the praying continued until the service reached its climax. Supported by the congregation, the cantor called out in high, penetrating tones: "Shemah Yisroel, Adoyshem Eloykheinu, Adoyshem echud" ("Hear o Israel, the Lord our God, the Lord is one"). And then softly: "Baruch Hashem kevoyd malchusoh l'aylom vo'eyd" ("Blessed is the name of His glorious kingdom forever and ever"). God was tangibly present in these harmonious sounds, and the country in which the faithful happened to live became as unimportant as the change of government.

> Lord of the world, King supreme,
> Ere aught was formed, He reigned alone.
> When by his will all things were wrought,
> Then was his sovereign name made known.
>
> And when in time all things shall cease,
> He still shall reign in majesty.
> He was, He is, He shall remain
> All-glorious eternally.
>
> Incomparable, unique is He,
> No other can His Oneness share.
> Without beginning, without end,
> Dominion's might is His to bear.
>
> He is my living God who saves,
> My Rock when grief or trials befall
> My Banner and my Refuge strong,
> My bounteous Portion when I call.
>
> My soul I give unto His care,
> Asleep, awake, for He is near,
> And with my soul, my body, too;
> God is with me, I have no fear.

Suddenly all was quiet. Only the folding of the chairs and the rustling of clothing could be heard as the men rose from their seats. Some exchanged smiles, others exchanged a few words. Visibly calm, ready to face the day ahead, they stepped out into the street and went on their way.

Shulim returned home. Along the way, he said hello to Duvid, who was hurrying to work, as he did every morning. When he arrived back home, Bezalel and Mottel were just swallowing the last of their breakfast. They grabbed their schoolbooks and took off with a hurried good-bye. Shulim joined Dvoire and Lemel at the table, still cluttered with the dishes the children had left in their rush. He took pleasure in those few quiet moments in the kitchen. The children's noise had ebbed, his wife was busy with the dishes and did not disturb him, and Lemel, as always, was sitting there without saying a word. Shulim could give free rein to his thoughts.

Were he and Dvoire happy? Had they ever thought about it? Probably not. Each had duties to fulfill that required them get along with each other. His was to father children who would follow in his footsteps; hers was to bear children and to raise them. That was enough to fill a lifetime. Seven of their nine offspring were sons, God be blessed. Life was to be lived, and should it also bring a little happiness in the bargain, then one was all the more grateful for the blessing. What did they talk about? They most likely discussed the business at her small tobacco and stationery shop, or whether the parents of one of his Talmud students still hadn't paid, or which *shadkhen*, matchmaker, they should engage to find a suitable match for Shayndl, who was already fourteen years old. Yes, Shayndl's wedding! Golde was, God be blessed, long married and had two daughters. Shayndl had just finished four years of basic schooling. Now she was apprenticed to a dressmaker. Sewing was a skill that would stand her in good stead once she was married, which would take place at the latest by the time she was sixteen. What was the *shadkhen*'s fee? How much of a dowry would she need? All these things had to be considered far in advance. Shulim was already over fifty and would not be able to support her forever.

Dvoire looked at the clock. "Golde's husband came by a while ago. Little Sure is ill, and Golde asked me to stop by and take a look at her. That's why I have to go now or I'll be late at the shop and the customers will find the door locked." While she spoke she put Lemel's little arms into the sleeves of his coat. Since the four-year-old was unable to walk, she carried him with her wherever she went. She already had the boy on her hip and her hand on the door handle when she smelled that the bucket, which always stood behind the curtain in the corridor, had not been emptied. Mottel and Bezalel are always fighting over whose turn it is to empty the bucket, and we have to put up with the smell, she thought, annoyed. Each one always claims it's the other's turn, and the bucket remains there untouched. I'll have to speak to them when they stop by at the shop after school, she thought as she opened the apartment door. She turned around once more and called to Shulim, "Don't forget to take your sandwiches." Shulim sighed. He, too, would have to leave soon, to go to cheder, the religious school. Teaching twenty four-, five-, and six-year-olds to read and write Hebrew wasn't easy. He could think of more interesting things to do with his time.

Shulim put on his coat and went back to shul. The classes started at 8:30. He left the dirty dishes where they were, of course. He knew that Shayndl would clean up and put everything away when she came home at four o'clock.

A smaller room next to the big hall of the synagogue served as cheder. The children were already there. Four long tables with equally long benches and a chalkboard in the corner were the only furnishings in the otherwise bare room. Some of the students were standing around in the middle of the room; others were already in their seats. As Shulim entered, the buzz of voices ceased. Everyone sat down and looked at him expectantly.

"Take out a sheet of paper. We are writing the whole alphabet, all *oissyes,* all letters." Some of the boys groaned. Again! "Only for twenty minutes, and then we'll read a *myseh,* a fairy tale," Shulim said to pacify them. He marched along the aisles, dictating. "Aleph, beis, gimmel, dalet, heh, vuv, zajin . . ." He broke off. "No, Duvid, this has to be longer, it looks like a yud. Ches, tes . . . Hershele," he asked suddenly, "what's the difference between shin and sin?" The boy looked at him unhappily. "You must have been asleep last time. Moishe, can you tell me?"

"The shin has the dot above the letter on the right, and the sin has it on the left," Moishe replied.

"Very good, Moishe. As a reward, you may read the first sentence of our fairy tale."

"How old are our *oissyes* and where do they come from? Who can tell me?" Shulim asked next.

"They are thousands of years old," called out seven-year-old Yome, "and they come from Palestine, only then it was called Israel." Shulim nodded with satisfaction.

Finally, when everyone had finished the exercise, they began to take out their Yiddish reading books. Although Yiddish is derived from German, it is the only language that is called Jewish. It is written in the same letters as the language of the prayers: Hebrew. For the children reading Yiddish, which they spoke at home and to each other, was like playing a game with letters.

"Today we'll read 'Gold and Iron' on page five. Moishe, begin."

The boy moved his finger from letter to letter, sounding them out until he suddenly recognized the whole word. "The metal gold wanted to get to know the world."

"And now you, Hershel," said Shulim.

One by one the boys read a sentence each. "It walked on and on. Suddenly it heard loud moaning and groaning. The metal gold halted its step. From afar it recognized a blacksmith in his shop, beating a glowing piece of iron with his hammer. With every blow, the iron wailed. 'What's all this complaining?' the gold asked the iron. 'All metals are hammered and forged. Even I, precious gold, I have been forged. Our fate is the same. I am highly valued and sought after by humans, but I still have to endure the same kind of hammering as you.' 'How can you compare our fates?' the iron called out bitterly. 'The hammer is made of iron, not gold! We may be able to bear the suffering a stranger inflicts on us, but I am being beaten by my own brother—and no pain can compare to that.'"

"Well, children, is that true?" Shulim asked.

Yome raised his hand. "I think if my big brother Lemel hits me, it hurts just as much as if Duvid did it. They're both strong." Several of the other boys agreed with him, but Hershel disagreed.

"The pain to the body is the same, that's true, but the pain to the soul is greater when the blows come from someone who belongs to your own family."

Shulim smiled, satisfied. "You may be asleep sometimes during the lessons, but when you're awake you have a sharp mind." The boys knew this was the highest praise. "Let's sing a song a song before we go."

"Oyfn Pripetchik!" Hershel called out. Shulim began to hum the familiar tune and motioned the class to join in.

Oyfn pripetchik brent a fayerl,
Un in shtib is heys
Un der rebbe lerent kleyne kinderlekh
Dem alef-bays.

Lernt zhe kinderlekh, hobt nisht keyne moyre,
Jeder onheib is shwer.
Glicklech is wer hot gelerent toyre,
Vus darf der mensh nokh mer.

Az ir vet kinderlekh elter vern,
Vet ir aleyn farshteyn,
Vifl in di oysyes lign trern,
Un vi fil geveyn.

Az ir vet, kinderlekh dem goles shlepn
Un oysgemutshet zayn,
Zolt ir fun di oysyes koyekh shepn,
Kukt in zey arayn.*

The children's voices easily followed the deep bass. Everybody knew this song well from home, where the whole family would often sing it together.

"That's it for today," said Shulim. The children needed no coaxing. They packed their books and quickly dispersed.

Shulim was glad to be alone again. It was half past ten and at two he had another class to teach. He wanted to rest for a while before doing his proofreading. A publisher had sent him a book, one of those silly women's stories. What's the name of the writer again? He pulled out the manuscript from his briefcase. Oh, yes, Sholem Alei-

---

*A flame is burning in the fireplace, the room warms up, as the teacher teaches the children the alef-beys: Learn, dear children, have no fear, for every beginning is hard. Happy is the one who learns Torah, what more can one want. When you grow older you will understand that this alphabet contains the tears and the weeping of our people. When you grow weary and burdened in exile, you will find comfort and strength within this Jewish alphabet.

chem. He poured a little tea from the samovar, unwrapped his lunch, and began to chew slowly on the bread.

About one o'clock, he put down his work. What he needed now was to stretch his legs and get some fresh air. He wanted to forget the images of this trivial world of love and conflicts, of poverty and daily chores, which the story forced on him. He needed this like a hole in the head. But he could not afford to refuse work. He took a deep breath as he turned into Legionov Boulevard, a few short steps away. The walk to Mickiewicz Square took fifteen minutes, but he was hardly aware of the crowd streaming around him, hurrying to some business or just taking a leisurely stroll. When he reached the square, he leaned against the wall of the most beautiful hotel in Lemberg. His eyes came to rest on the statue of Adam Mickiewicz in the middle of the square. His view was obstructed, however, by the ceaseless procession of horse-drawn carriages—and those new monsters called automobiles—passing by. The entrance door of the hotel was constantly opening and closing as elegant ladies and gentlemen came and went. Through the curtains covering the huge windows of the café, Shulim could make out indistinct figures seated at the tables. How much he would have liked to go in, to have a piece of cake and coffee. Sighing, he tore himself away and quickened his step. As he passed Dvoire's shop, he glanced through the window. She was waiting on a customer. He hurried past. She is a good wife, even though I never felt the kind of passion for her that I . . . He forced himself to break off the thought. Whenever his thoughts turned to the love of his youth he became restless. He had never dared to tell his parents about her. When he finally had mustered his courage, it had been too late. The marriage contract with Dvoire's parents had already been signed. The Talmud says: "It is good that we should raise our children and be saved from transgression." If this was good enough for the great sages, it is good enough for me, he reprimanded himself.

Shortly before two, he was back in shul. The students began to arrive one by one; two were still missing. These boys were already twelve years old. In another year they would be called up to the bimah on Shabbes like grown men during their bar mitzvah celebrations and would be allowed to read from the Torah in front of the community.

The cheder was buzzing with voices. Some students were swaying back and forth in prayer, chanting out loud. Marks were given not only for learning God's laws and their various interpretations of the last two thousand years; the students also learned both to ask questions and to call into question, that is, they learned to think or *trachten* as one says in Yiddish. The best student was the one who gave an intelligent interpretation that was valid for the present and was able to defend it most convincingly. That is why many Jews habitually answer a question with a counterquestion. When the two stragglers came in five minutes late, Shulim said, annoyed, "Please, try to be on time," but then decided that nothing would be gained by making a fuss about it.

"Let's begin. Shloime, Purim comes in a month. Where do we find the story of the event that is celebrated?"

"In the Tanakh."

"Good. Duvid, what does the Tanakh consist of?"

"The Torah, which are the five books of Moses, and then the Histories, the Prophets, and the Writings. The Book of Esther is part of the Writings. This is the story we tell on Purim."

Shloime, a delicate boy with blond hair, sat there more quietly than usual. "Reb Zwerling," he said suddenly, "when we enter the shul we say: 'Through your abundant kindness I come into your House, I prostrate myself before your holy sanctuary in fear of you.' Again and again, we express in our prayers joy that we may fear God. But when I'm afraid, I can't feel joy, and I couldn't love somebody I'm afraid of."

Shulim nodded his head. "Well, you know, this is a question of translation, a matter of meaning. In Hebrew, the word is *yir'os*. But this is not fear; it is awe as in *yir'os hakoved,* holy fear."

The boy frowned.

"Yes, yes, you're right," Shulim continued. "Look here, He freed us from slavery in Egypt and performed signs and wonders to save us. He is a benevolent father, but He also demands of us that we keep His laws. Just look for a moment at the Ten Commandments, which Moishe brought down from Mount Sinai for the people of Israel. If you study the writings properly, you will discover that people need rules to guide them. Remember the dance around the golden calf. Many of our people behaved like animals."

The class was silent.

Nuchem began to speak, hesitated, almost stammered. He felt that he was about to touch on a taboo: "Reb Zwerling . . . how does one know that God exists, I mean, if one can never see or touch Him . . . ?"

Shulim's face darkened. Angry, he called out, "If you don't feel Him, then I feel sorry for you and there is no place for you here." His voice rose, he became increasingly agitated, and he forgot that he was talking to a child. He seemed to think he was speaking to one of the young men his son Uri brought home sometimes. They want to work on the Shabbes. Whether they eat kosher or *treife* is all the same to them. They adopt the customs of the goyim, dress like them, and believe they will be happier that way. "Do you want to join the goyim, who have robbed and killed us for centuries? Or maybe the materialists? They seem to think they can do everything with reason. They will come to a bitter end. Without awe of God, you have no awe of men. If you don't believe in Him, you not only lose respect for yourself and others, you become like driftwood in the sea. Such people end up at each other's throats, Nuchem!"

He thundered the last sentence. To the students, he appeared like God himself, with his droning bass and fiery eyes. When he heard himself calling the boy's name, however, Shulim came to his senses. He patted the boy's head, overcome with pity for him, as if his doubts had already condemned him to be lost.

"You're still young. If you study hard, you'll find the answer to your question by yourself . . ."

When Shayndl returned home in the afternoon, she would hold her breath and quicken her step in the passageway, even before she reached the inner courtyard. She had to pass the toilet that served the entire building, and she hated the ghastly stench. Longingly she recalled having heard that in the beautiful hotel on Mickiewicz Square each floor had at least two toilets, one for men, one for women. When she reached the apartment, she took off her coat quickly and cleared the table. The dishes for *milchiges* and *fleishiges* had to be washed separately. She stacked them next to two large basins, took a bucket, filled it with water from the faucet in the stairway, and then placed it on the iron stove. With the help of some paper and a few pieces of wood, she made a fire. While she was washing the dishes, she began to sing as she usually did to break the boredom of the chore. She sang, her voice rising and sinking, clear and pure.

In those days, Yiddish folk songs were often heard from many windows, sometimes in different versions, but all the songs told stories of daily life, of love, of expulsions. Some were filled with mourning, others with mockery and humor.

Shayndl abruptly broke off in the midst of a long vibrato tone. "Hello, Papa," she called out, and turned toward her father, who was just then opening the apartment door.

Shulim's heart warmed at the sound of her voice. He delighted in the beauty of his daughter's dark eyes and her thick, wavy, brown hair. Shayndl, the beautiful, he thought.* Yes, the name fits her. In a year, she will be the same age as Dvoire was when we got married. I'll find her a good husband, one who will make her happy. He greeted her with a light touch on the shoulder. "Please make me some tea, I'll lie down for a while."

"Yes, Papa." Shayndl put more water on the stove and took out the teapot and a cup. When the *milchige* dishes were done, she called out, "Mottel!" Her eleven-year-old brother was in the next room doing his homework and did not budge. He could easily guess why she was calling him. He was still too young to refuse to do women's work. But he was looking forward to his bar mitzvah. Then nobody would demand such things of him anymore.

"Mottel!" Shayndl was getting impatient.

"Quiet!" The sudden boom of her father's voice startled her.

Mottel reluctantly got out of his chair and came into the kitchen. "I'm coming," he muttered. He knew better than to arouse his father's anger.

He took one of the dish towels from the hook and took three plates from the pile all at once.

"You're using the *fleishige* towel," Shayndl said impatiently, and placed the right one in his hand. "And don't take so many plates at once. You dropped one the other day."

This stupid cow, Mottel thought. Papa permits her to wrap him

Shayn is the Yiddish word for "beautiful."

around her little finger, just because she is a girl. She doesn't have to sit over a book all the time as I do, and now she acts as if she were my teacher. "Shayndl, di shayne, Shayndl, di shayne!" he teased her. He danced around with his arms extended and pretended he was about to let the three plates slip from his hands.

"Will you stop it, you jerk," she grumbled. The more she showed her anger, the more wildly and loudly he carried on. Now Shayndl snatched the plates from him to rescue them. "Stop it!" she hollered.

The two were still fighting over the plates when Shulim suddenly appeared in the doorway. His face was angry. "I said I want quiet." He spoke softly, but to the children it seemed as if the clouds had opened, accompanied by rolling thunder.

The rattling of the boiling kettle burst into the tense silence. "Yes, Papa," Shayndl said quickly. "I'll bring your tea right away."

Shulim went back out, leaving the door open so that Shayndl could follow him. Mottel, meanwhile, put down the three plates and began to dry them one by one, and after that took only one at a time.

When Shayndl brought her father the cup of tea, she found him stretched out on the couch. "Thank you, my child," he said wearily, and gave her a light pat on the hand. She sighed with relief. He was no longer angry. She held back a sudden impulse to kiss his cheek, for this would not have been proper. Demonstrative tenderness was rare in this family. Only Uri would sometimes hug her in a moment of spontaneous good cheer. Shayndl went back into the kitchen. Without another word, the children finished the dishes. Then Mottel returned to his homework. Shayndl started setting the table. Soon her brothers would be coming home. And, of course, their mother, Dvoire.

❀

Dvoire—1910

Dvoire opened her little shop exactly on time, as always, hoping that the customers would leave her at least fifteen minutes to herself. She had been too tired yesterday to sweep the floor. She placed the boy in a child's chair at the small table. Suddenly she remembered the shelves. They still needed to be dusted and straightened. It was a good thing that the light from the window did not reach the back of the long, narrow shop. The dust on the rear shelves was not visible when only the front light was lit.

She sighed. It was early morning and she already felt tired. Could she be harboring some illness? Shulim sometimes said that she was suffering from sleeping disease. But she could not afford to be ill.

She placed paper and colored pencils on the table before Lemel. "Draw something, draw a picture," she said, stroking his head. He could sit for hours without making a sound, completely withdrawn within himself. It was easy to forget that he was there. She regretted nothing more bitterly than what she had done to this boy. Would eight children not have been enough? When the ninth announced itself, everything within her rebelled against this child. She consulted one of those backstreet abortionists, paid good money for some evil-smelling brew, and prayed for the child to disappear. But it resisted all her efforts and came into the world. And what kind of child did it turn out to be . . .

She took the broom and began to sweep. Her thoughts wandered to business matters. She had sold the last tin of the strongest Luntin pipe tobacco and would have to order more. And the supply of notebooks was getting low. The picture of little Sure's feverish red face intruded on her thoughts. Golde would nurse the child back to health without help from an expensive doctor, she reassured herself. She just would have to apply the cold compresses to the child's calves, as she had shown her, and the fever would no doubt come down. A little warm milk with butter and sugar would soothe the aching throat.

It certainly would be a big help if business were to pick up a little today so she could afford some honey, she thought. If only it were that easy to cure our Lemel. She sighed. The doctors spoke of brain damage and told her, "He will never learn to speak or walk. It would be best for the child if you placed him in a home. He would be with others like himself, and the nurses would take care of him." She refused. Something told her that this child needed constant attention. Her older children didn't need her anymore and the younger ones had each other. Lemel had only her.

She looked around and her gaze fell on the typewriter standing on the counter. A salesman had talked her into it yesterday. "All you have to do is display it for everyone to see. If you sell it, you'll get a 5 percent commission." Since she had nothing to lose, she agreed. The day she sold it would be her lucky day.

She put the broom away and looked at Lemel's drawings. Always green lines, long lines and short lines, spaced with amazing regularity. The doctor had suggested that she show him how to make a circle. She had tried, but he had only watched her and then continued drawing straight lines. "Well done," she said mechanically, as she looked over her stock and bent over her order form.

The doorbell rang. A boy of about ten entered the shop. She could see from the way he was dressed that his mother did not have to turn over every penny. He asked for a penholder in a medium price range, one that would not break too easily. Could he afford this because in his family there were only a few children?

She overcame her reticence about asking such a personal question. "How many brothers and sisters do you have?"

The boy was obviously surprised by this strange woman's interest, but answered readily, "I have one older sister."

"No more?" The boy shook his head. One of her mother's sayings, which she had never understood, came into her mind: "A mama is a mother, but a child is a mosquito." Dvoire suddenly understood its meaning: The child sucks and sucks until the mother is sucked dry. Yes, this is what she felt. If she had only two children instead of nine, she wouldn't always be so tired. But as she looked at Lemel she felt like a criminal to even have had that thought. She gave the boy his change, and he left.

Soon she had finished filling out the order form. Since business

was still quiet, she switched on the rear ceiling lamp and carried
Lemel with his chair and table to the back of the shop. She gathered
a stack of notebooks of various sizes, took a box of colored pencils
from the shelf, spread it all out before him, and explained the
names of the colors and the sizes and shapes of the objects. This is
what the doctor had told her to do. Lemel looked at her but showed
no interest. Was she wasting her energy? She did not know and continued. She dusted each object before returning it to the shelf. She
had just finished dusting three shelves of merchandise and had put
the rag back into the drawer when the door opened again. It was
her son Duvid, who was a tailor's apprentice.

"Hello, Mama. The boss needs two receipt pads."

"Of course. I'm glad to see you. Please pick up two pounds of
onions, one bulb of garlic, and two pounds of apples on the way
home, will you?" She took the money from the register. He nodded.
Dvoire knew she could rely on him.

Duvid was barely gone when Mrs. Grinberg entered the shop.
"Mrs. Zwerling, look at this." She held up an envelope, her eyes
shining. "My son wrote from America and put in a fifty-dollar bill.
Just imagine, he's getting married!" Her face turned sad. "But I
won't be able to go. He can't afford to pay for the passage, and I certainly can't either. I wonder, will I ever see my daughter-in-law? Or
my grandchildren?" She sighed.

Dvoire looked at her sympathetically. "It's bitter when the children are so far away."

"But I didn't come here to complain. I need paper and an envelope so I can write to my son. And since you're a businesswoman,
maybe you can tell me where I can get money for these American
dollars?"

Dvoire put the requested items in front of her. "Just go down
Legionov Boulevard toward Mickiewicz Square. On the right you'll
see a large bank. I'm sure they'll be able to exchange the money for
you."

As Mrs. Grinberg left, the next customer held the door for her.

"Mrs. Friedmann!" Dvoire called out in surprise. "I haven't seen
you for a long time. How have you been?"

"Oh, Mrs. Zwerling, haven't you heard about my son? He's in
the hospital. He was attacked by one of those razor-blade gangs.

They left him bleeding in the street. He lost a lot of blood, thirteen deep cuts . . ."

Dvoire's face turned ashen. This could easily happen to her sons, too. "Did you report it to the militia?"

The woman nodded. "If they wanted to, they could have brought these gangs under control long ago. But since they only attack Jews, the militia is not interested. One gets the impression from some of those policemen that they wouldn't mind taking part themselves. Nuchem recognized one of the young men. His father is one of your customers, Mr. Benkowski from the tax office."

Dvoire's eyes widened. This was the customer who always bought new and expensive pipes. He must have twenty of them, unless he constantly loses them.

"Nuchem is still in bed. But he wants to write to the press about it. That's why I'm here. I need a writing pad."

The bell rang again. The two women turned toward the door and then looked at each other, startled. Speak of the devil and there he is, Dvoire thought as she breathed in deeply to ease the tenseness in her chest. She waited on Mrs. Friedmann, who then quickly disappeared.

Dvoire turned away for a moment to steady her beating heart. Then she put on her best smile and looked firmly at the customer.

"Mr. Benkowski, how can I help you?"

"I would like a pipe."

"Of course, Mr. Benkowski, I'll show you what I have."

Does he know what his son is doing? The father, at least, was always courteous. She spread out her assortment of pipes on the counter before him.

He picked up the best and most expensive piece, holding it in his hand with obvious appreciation. He looked at the price, thought for a moment, and remarked, "This one is very nice, but I can't afford so much. Since you Jews like to bargain, I'll offer you half the price."

That's all I need! Dvoire thought. If I refuse, I may feel it next time my taxes fall due. Cautiously she said, "I don't like bargaining, Mr. Benkowski. These are the fair prices. If I go below, it'll be a loss for me."

"Since I'm such a good customer, couldn't you do me this one favor?" he insisted. "Everybody knows how rich you Jews are. I have a cash flow problem at the moment, and I really like this pipe." He named a sum that was still considerably below the marked price.

Despite her fear of this public official's power and the violence of his son, Dvoire shook her head. If she were to give in now, he would demand a reduced price for expensive items every time. "We're not rich, Mr. Benkowski. Look at this pipe," she said, holding up a less expensive one, "it's also very nice."

"Yes, my dear woman, that's how one gets on in life, by being tough. That's how you all got rich. All right, give me that pipe." She wrapped it in her finest tissue paper.

"Might you be needing some tobacco with it?" she asked with an exaggeratedly polite smile.

"Let me have one tin of the strongest sort of that English tobacco you always have."

"I'm sorry but I'm just all out of the strongest Luntin. I could sell you the medium or light sort."

"No, no. Forget it. That'll be all."

Dvoire's knees trembled slightly when he was gone. She had to sit down on the stool behind the counter. What will she do if he makes difficulties when she files her taxes? Or what if his son's gang were to vandalize her shop! She preferred not to think about it. No. No matter what the consequences, one can't just take everything they dish out. To distract herself, she turned to her son. Green lines again. She put a red pencil in his hand. "Why don't you try this color?" she said. She felt a pinch of hunger and unpacked the lunch she had brought for Lemel and herself: bread with chicken fat.

In the next few hours she waited on several customers who made minor purchases. She was relieved when she had placed her order with the salesman who stopped by on his round. About three Uri came bolting into the shop.

"Mama, I have somebody for the typewriter," he called out excitedly. "Is it still here?"

A well-dressed young man followed him. "Mama, this is Marek Belyonski. His father is a lawyer, and he studies law, too. He also writes for *Wschod*. His father wants to give him the typewriter for his birthday. Isn't this wonderful?"

Dvoire nodded. She did not want to show too openly how

delighted she was, and asked soberly, "Do you have any idea at all how to use it, young man?"

"But certainly, and what I don't know my father's secretary will explain to me."

He had the money right in his pocket and was ready to take the machine with him. It was not until he had left the shop with the machine and she had placed the money in the register that Dvoire thought of asking, "Uri, how do you know such a student?"

"From Poale Zion."

Dvoire shook her head. Shulim did not like to see his children getting involved in such worldly affairs. It was bad enough for him that he was forced to send his children to public school for four years, taking time away from their religious studies. She decided not to tell her husband anything about the student. Suddenly she remembered, "Uri, when you see Mottel, tell him the bucket has to be emptied or there will be a terrible ruckus when I get home."

Uri grinned. "When you make a ruckus, Mama, that's just a pat on the head for him. But I'll give him the message."

"Uri, can you get a jar of honey and take it to Golde for sick little Surele?"

He nodded. She opened the register and handed him the money. Her next words came out soft and haltingly, "I'm very grateful to you for bringing a customer for the typewriter."

Praise and recognition were rare in the family, and her own words made her feel embarrassed.

"D . . . don't . . . mention it," Uri stammered in surprise and left the shop.

Her eyes caught the open register and she felt satisfied. This sale opened new possibilities. The salesman said he would be back the following week. Now she could ask him to bring another machine. Suddenly she was overcome with fatigue and longed to lie down. Lemel's head was tipped forward over the table, his arms dangling. He was fast asleep. She leaned back in her chair and closed her eyes. Her thoughts raced through her head. She would do many things differently if she could start all over again.

She had seen Shulim twice before the wedding—the first time through a keyhole when his parents and the matchmaker introduced him to her parents; the second time over tea and cake after their parents had agreed on the terms and had signed the marriage contract. The dowry had been enough for her to open this shop. She knew her parents had meant well. He had been twenty-eight and she fifteen. Within the Jewish world, she would enjoy greater honor with a poor religious scholar than if she had married a rich man. Actually, Shulim had not displeased her. He was slender, had raven-black, wavy hair, and was a head taller than she. She was most impressed by his dark penetrating eyes. But what had she known then about marriage, getting pregnant, and having children? My God, how naive and ignorant I was, she thought, as she recalled her wedding day.

The wedding was probably the best thing about the whole marriage, although, even then, she had sat shy and withdrawn between Shulim and her parents and only dared to stir when she was spoken to. Her father practically had to force the wine on her. "You look as if you're at a funeral rather than at your wedding," he said. And when the more than three hundred guests urged her to dance, she followed Shulim with stiff steps. She felt like a puppet that had been wound up the wrong way.

She had been frightened of the unknown. She had felt the pressure to form a family, to have children. That they grew inside the belly and came out after nine months she had learned from watching her mother. But how did they get there? She did not know and did not dare to ask.

After the wedding party, alone with Shulim in the bedroom, she had sat lost on the edge of the bed. He sat down next to her, put his arm around her, and gave her a kiss on the cheek. Then he rose abruptly and began to speak in a businesslike manner: "Put on your nightgown. We're going to bed." It was years later that she realized he had hidden his own uncertainty behind the matter of fact tone. Back then, her fear had only intensified, and she did as she was told. He pressed his body against hers and began to caress her. Then he pushed something hard that she had never seen before between her thighs. He moved quickly back and forth, got increasingly excited, and suddenly she felt some sticky fluid on her skin. Then he let out a deep moan and sank back on the bed. He kissed her once more on the cheek and wiped off the fluid with a piece of cloth he had kept hidden. "Every beginning is difficult, but it'll get easier, Dvoire," he said. As time passed, her fear left her and she became pregnant. She became a mother, first twice in a row, then at regular intervals of two to three years. He always seemed to enjoy their nighttime encounters more than she did, but she had become used to that long ago.

A noise startled her from her thoughts. Lemel had woken up. "Ahh, ahh," he bayed, and stuck out his tongue. Dvoire shook off her fatigue. He was thirsty. Two more hours until closing time. Then it would be home to the family, cooking, getting after the children to do their chores, and finally to bed. If only I could have a few days in bed, she thought, as the doorbell rang and the next customer entered the shop.

Shayndl and Uri—1910

A t the supper table, the whole family gathered around. Dvoire told the story of how Nuchem Friedmann had been stabbed by the razor-blade gang. She looked imploringly at her sons. "You be careful. When you see a gang of thugs in the street, cross over to the other side. And you two," she turned to Uri and Mottel, "I forbid you to get into any squabbles."

She knew Mottel's eagerness to defend himself, even if the odds were against him. And Uri had a deeply ingrained sense of justice, which often got him into trouble.

"Yes, Mama," said Uri. "I promise. But still, we can't always run away like dogs with our tails between our legs. We must find a dignified solution." He did not dare continue, for he knew what was coming.

"When the Moshiach comes, Uri, he will redeem us and lead us back to Jerusalem. Then these problems will be solved, not before!" said Shulim in a sharp tone. Everybody around the table perceived the underlying reprimand, warning his son not to associate with the *shaygetzen,* the heretics, who deign to take fate into their own hands by establishing a worldly Jewish state in Palestine, without waiting for the coming of the Moshiach, without God.

"Yes, Father," said Uri, and kept his peace. It was senseless to discuss this topic. Too many heated debates had already taken place around the family table. Uri had even brought home older friends, hoping they could persuade his father, but in vain. What Uri really held against his father was the way he treated him—as if he were an ignorant child, incapable of forming his own opinions. The father usually ate dinner in silence and did not participate in the discussions, but when he spoke, he always had the last word, and no one was allowed to challenge it. Why can't he see that times have changed? Uri often wondered in exasperation.

Uri was the first to get up from the table. "Where are you going?" asked Dvoire.

He answered with a dismissive gesture. "I'm going for a walk, just window shopping."

But Dvoire's thoughts were already elsewhere, and she did not notice the obvious lie. Only Shayndl was curious, and she accompanied her brother to the street.

"Where are you really going?" she asked. He grinned, and she had to promise to keep it to herself.

"Poale Zion has a meeting tonight. Several of us want to go to Palestine. Nobody will humiliate us there, and we'll get away from the narrowness of this ghetto." His words almost took Shayndl's breath away. Uri saw that he had shocked her.

"Shayndl," he beseeched her, "I don't want to go on living like our parents. Everywhere in the world there is development. Factories are being built, sewer systems are being laid, electricity is produced, there are telephones, phonographs, automobiles. But we live cut off from any progress, and not only because the Poles won't let us attend secondary schools, but also because of our own laws that chain us to the Middle Ages." He spoke with great intensity. "Just take the Sabbath. If we insist on keeping Saturday as the holy day of rest while the others have their Sunday, is it any wonder that the factories don't want to hire Jews?"

Shayndl nodded with a troubled look. She saw his point, but she could not go against her parents. Uri guessed her thoughts.

"You're a good girl," he said with an ironic smile. He bent over and gave her a light kiss on the cheek. She pushed him away, annoyed.

Suddenly their attention was drawn to a child screaming in the street. A woman was pulling a bawling Polish boy of about five by the hand. "You'd better come, now. You can't play with Katya now. It's dark and we have to go home. Everybody is waiting for us, and Grandpa will be angry. After supper you can play as much as you want." The boy calmed down, but he did not budge.

Shayndl waited to see what would happen next. The father, who had been standing next to the boy, took his hand and said, "If you don't come now, the Jews will come at Easter, cut your throat, and use your blood for making their matzah." The boy looked horrified at his father, swallowed his tears, and unwillingly let himself be pulled along.

Shayndl and Uri looked at each other without a word. He shook his head, and she, almost inaudibly, let out a Yiddish curse: "May the earth swallow them up." They exchanged an understanding glance and parted. Uri was the only one of her brothers with whom she could speak freely; often they understood each other without words.

Uri arrived at the apartment and rang the bell. No one would have taken him for seventeen. With his tall, slender figure, bushy brows, and full beard, he looked more like a man of twenty. A young woman opened the door.

"Shalom, Rosa."

"Take off your coat, quickly. We're about to begin." The clothes hook was buried under piles of coats and jackets. Uri looked around.

"Over here." Rosa pointed to the dresser on which several men's overcoats had already been placed. Together they entered the living room packed with young people. Some were sitting on chairs, some on pillows on the floor, and others just leaning against the wall. The sofa and two upholstered chairs had been ceded to the few older men present. Uri sought out a spot near the wall so that he would not disturb the speaker, Rosa's father.

"It is impossible to fight anti-Semitism, because anti-Semitism is an irrational fear of the devil and a mass psychosis that is thousands of years old. I often encounter cases of psychosis in my clinical practice, and it is rare that such a person is cured. The entire Jewish people will always be held responsible for the transgressions of a few individual Jews. When a Pole commits a robbery, nobody thinks of calling all Poles robbers. But they say we crucified Jesus, we drink the blood of Christians, we poison wells, despite the fact that it has been proven time and again that these are fabrications, slanders. Come the next social upheaval, and we will again be blamed, our blood will be shed, our homes destroyed, and we will be driven out altogether. Either we have the strength to contain these sinister forces or we have to get out of their way."

He picked up a book and read the title out loud: "*Autoemancipation: A Warning to His Fellows by a Russian Jew.* As early as 1882, Leo Pinsker had made clear in this book that assimilation was senseless. We have only one way out. We must find the way back to ourselves . . ."

The man next to him interjected, "But not by submerging ourselves in religion. The way out is through physical work in our own
land. We have been excluded from agriculture for centuries. Many
of our fellows waste away in a stifling *stibl*. The general trend in
society is toward strengthening the working class, but we have hardly any part in it. In our own land, we can live the way any normal
people lives. Just imagine, in such a country a Jewish policeman
would arrest a Jewish thief."

General laughter. The speaker nodded with satisfaction. The
thought of a Jewish policeman seemed absurd to everyone present.

Rosa's father spoke again. "For all you latecomers, I want to
introduce Ber Borochow." He pointed to the man who had just
spoken. Uri was deeply impressed to see the well-known ideologue
of Poale Zion, the Jewish socialist workers' movement, in the flesh.
"He will address a public meeting here in Lemberg the day after
tomorrow. All those who want to emigrate to Palestine will have an
opportunity to sign up." Uri nodded. Would he sign up now? If his
father were to hear of it, all hell would break loose at home. No, he
could not yet commit himself openly. A year ago one of his friends
disappeared without a trace, and only six months later did his family find out that he was in Palestine. He could not do that to his parents. What he would do was prepare for his departure secretly, but
he would tell his family the truth and say good-bye when he was
ready to leave.

A date for the next meeting was set before they adjourned. "We
still have a few copies of *Autoemancipation* left for sale," said Rosa's
father.

Uri sighed. He could not afford it. As everyone was standing
around, continuing the discussion in small clusters, he tapped Rosa
on the shoulder. "Could you lend me the book?" he asked.

The next evening, Shayndl had just finished setting the table
when Uri came into the kitchen.

"Who's at home?" he asked, almost in a whisper.

"Papa. He's asleep," she replied. He nodded, pleased, and sat
down on the chair in the corner where the light was best for reading
the book he pulled from his pocket.

"What are you reading?" Shayndl asked. He held up the spine of
the book and placed his finger on his lips, pointing in the direction
of where their father was.

"What does 'autoemancipation' mean?" Shayndl asked.

"Self-liberation."

Shayndl frowned.

"It's a really wonderful book." Uri's eyes shone with enthusiasm. He pointed to a paragraph. "Here, read this."

"Our fatherland—foreign soil, our unity—the dispersion, our solidarity—general hostility, our weapon—humility, our defense—accommodation, our future—the next day. What a despicable role for a people that once had its Maccabees!"

Shayndl had never read or heard such words. She read them over. Foreign soil, general hostility, and demeaning humility: Was that not her life, too? She felt it, but she would not have been able to express it like that. The words impressed themselves into her brain.

"Ber Borochow will speak at a public meeting tomorrow. Do you want to come?" Again Shayndl looked at him apprehensively. "Just tell them you're going to see Miriam to work on a pattern for a new dress."

Shayndl was torn between her parents' expectations and her own desires. She just could not rebel against her parents like her big brother. But Uri's talk about his plans for the future kindled in her a hope that made her feel alive as never before. She knew that she had to resist or she would end up like her mother. She would be married within a year and soon thereafter have her first child. Her parents were already searching for a suitable husband. No! Everything in her revolted against such a life. She wanted to make her own choice, select the man she would marry herself. And under no circumstances would she have nine children like her mother! She was determined not to continue this tradition. At most she would have two. Now, however, she shook her head. "Go without me, but tell me how it went. And, you know, I'd like to read that book."

Uri nodded. "Just don't let Papa find it."

The hall was filled almost to capacity when Uri arrived. A leaflet was handed to him at the entrance. He looked around. In the front row he recognized Marek Belyonski and several other familiar faces from his group. He made his way toward them, and they moved closer together to make room for him. He glanced at the leaflet. "Fundamental Propositions of the World Jewish Socialist Workers' Association Poale Zion," the headline read. "The Jewish Socialist

Workers' Association Poale Zion, as part of the international prole-
tariat, aims, in solidarity with the latter, to abolish the capitalist
economic order and to establish a socialist society."

The shrill, impatient sound of the bell made all eyes turn toward
the podium. The speaker was seated at a long table covered with a
red cloth. The chairman waited for the noise to die down, then he
officially opened the meeting. "You received the aims of Poale Zion
at the entrance. These are the resolutions passed at the Second
World Conference in December 1909. It is my pleasure to welcome
tonight two of the main speakers at that conference. Ber Borochow
will address the assembly first."

Applause rose and then died down quickly when Borochow
began to speak. Uri listened attentively. He did not understand
everything that was said, but one thing was clear to him: The Jews
were poor because they were incapable of adjusting to industrializa-
tion. The many family workshops could not possibly compete with
the large-scale factories. "National competition is not the result of
some machination on the part of a few bad, egotistical men of the
ruling class; it is the result of the developing, capitalist economy,
which inexorably drives toward expansion." This sounded logical
and conformed with what had been discussed in the group: The
Jews can only be part of this expansion if they cease to be a people
of the book and become workers of the soil and of the hand. Uri
glanced at the leaflet, letting himself be distracted for a moment.
Poale Zion was seeking a territorial solution to the Jewish question,
he read, by establishing economic enterprises based on cooperative
principles in Palestine. Uri's attention was drawn back to the platform by Borochow's urgent tone.

"A realistic nationalism does not dream of preservation of traditions, it does not seek to magnify them, it is not deceived by apparent national unity, it understands the class structure of society, and
does not attempt to gloss over the true interests of various groups.
This nationalism seeks the true liberation of the nation through
normalization of the conditions of production."

Again rousing applause. Uri clapped his hands again and again,
sitting upright, his head held high. It was an exciting, exalting feeling to be one with so many people.

"Shayndl," said Shulim, "tomorrow we'll start rehearsing the

Purim play. Please come to shul at five."

"Papa, don't you think I'm too old for this? I turned fifteen last month," she reminded him.

He stroked her hair gently. "Next year, my child, we'll pick another princess. This year you're still my child." He emphasized the last two words, and although he had already begun looking for a husband for her, he realized how painful it was for him to accept the fact that his daughter would leave him one day.

Shayndl was torn between two desires. On the one hand, she no longer looked like a child. Her breasts had begun to swell when she was only nine, and by now they were no smaller than those of her sister, who was twelve years older. At eleven she had begun to menstruate. She felt it was ridiculous for her to still be a part of this children's play. On the other hand, she loved the story of Esther and enjoyed acting in it. Well, all right. Soon she would have to insist on seeking and finding happiness in her own way. But at this point, she was not yet ready to confront her parents. How often she had wished that they could be more open to her questions and thoughts. For example, what purpose was served by all the hard work of keeping a kosher household? Four or five thousand years ago, in the desert, when water was scarce and it was difficult to keep food and oneself clean, it certainly made sense. But here, in Europe, today, when water came out of pipes inside the house? And wouldn't it be better to have three children at most? Children don't die as often as they did in the old days. And the clothing restrictions! Shayndl always wanted to know the reason for everything that was demanded of her. Only then was she willing to keep traditions. She did not realize that in doing so she was following an ancient Jewish tradition, that is, questioning traditions and at the same time clinging to them to a point where they become dogma. But she could share such thoughts only with Uri and her friend Leah. Her parents turned a deaf ear whenever she tried to ask such questions. Shayndl then had the feeling that she did not exist, that she had not spoken at all.

She remembered one silent struggle, when her persistence actually broke through Dvoire's deafness. She was eleven years old and one day she went home with Leah, her best friend in school. Shayndl was amazed when she entered the apartment. "Four rooms for only three people?" she said. Leah had no brothers and sisters, and her father was an engineer. Shayndl stood in the middle of the room and took everything in. The furniture was carefully matched, not thrown together haphazardly because it was cheap, as it was at her house.

"Do you really have this room all to yourself?" She could hardly believe it.

On the bed, dolls and stuffed animals were grouped around a little pillow in a bright wine-red and cobalt-blue velvet case. Shayndl looked at it, unable to turn her eyes away from it. Hesitantly, almost reverently, she brushed her hand over the soft fabric.

"That's my cuddling pillow," Leah said. "I have to hold it in my arms or I can't go to sleep." Shayndl sighed. Her parents could not afford to buy dolls and stuffed animals, but such a pillow, surely that would be possible.

At home, Shayndl said to Dvoire, "Mama, I would like to have a little pillow in a velvet case."

Her mother was in the process of scrubbing a burned pot, and Shayndl had apparently cut into her train of thought. She turned a puzzled look at her daughter. "What do you need such *schmonzes* for? Where should I get velvet?"

"But the pillow needn't be big, maybe thirty centimeters, and that requires very little velvet."

Dvoire just couldn't, no, *wouldn't* be bothered with such nonsense. But after a week of stubborn begging and pleading from her daughter, Dvoire begrudgingly gave in, and two weeks later Shayndl had her pillow. But the persistent pain of not existing when she asked existential questions concerning the future was unbearable. Since she was unable to make herself heard, she just stopped asking her parents such questions.

When Shayndl got to shul the next day, she found her father and five students from his bar mitzvah class with their books open in front of them, as well as several younger boys and girls.

"King Ahasverus prepared a feast," Yome was explaining as she entered, "and on the seventh day, in high spirits from the wine, he ordered his queen, Vashti by name, to appear before everybody to show off her beauty. But she refused. The king's advisers counseled him to disown her, because if word got around, all wives would refuse to do as they were told. His new queen was Esther. She was an orphan who had been raised by her uncle, Mordechai. He told her that she'd better not tell anybody that she was Jewish, so nobody in the palace knew."

Even though Shayndl had heard this story and acted in the play every year for ten years, it seemed to her as if she were hearing it for the first time. It was the first time she was able to put herself in the place of these two women. Right she was, that Vashti, Shayndl thought. Why should she exhibit herself in front of a bunch of wanton drunkards? What a disgusting man to demand something like that of his wife! And Esther? She wasn't asked whether or not she wanted to be queen. Just as I'm not being asked whom I want to marry. She would have liked to read the story by herself and wished she could read Hebrew like her brothers. The bitterness of an old wound rose in her.

She had been six years old. Her father had permitted her to accompany him and her brothers to cheder. She had been excited in anticipation and had looked forward to learning when they left the apartment, but when they had reached the gate of the synagogue, her father had turned to her and said, "Well, Shayndl, you were allowed to come along. Now be good and go back home."

She had looked at him with bitter disappointment. "But Papa, I want to learn to read, write, and think, too," she said.

Even after all this time, she could still hear her brothers' laughter. Her father had placed his hand lovingly on her shoulder. "But Shayndl, this is not for girls. Run home quickly and play, or help Mama with cooking so dinner will be ready when we get home." Helpless and unable to disobey him, she had turned and gone away. From afar, she had watched the others, still chattering, disappear inside the shul. Even now, when she saw the boys with their books, she again felt as excluded and rejected as she had then.

The Purim players were gathered in a room next to the sanctuary. Shayndl was overcome with a bittersweet longing as she put on her Queen Esther costume. This was the last time and thus a goodbye to her childhood. Duvid held up a black pencil and asked her to draw a mustache for him. Several mothers of younger children used pieces of fabric, shawls, and safety pins to transform the girls into palace servants and boys into sentries. Yome wrapped a sash tightly around his waist and stuck a cardboard sword into it. Shulim opened the door and took a peek into the auditorium. The room was filled with the din of voices, which ceased abruptly. Shulim was excited, even elated, when he announced: "There are about eight hundred people. Hurry up, children, five minutes until curtain time."

In the corners of a stage in the center of the hall a throne, a gate, and gallows had been erected. All the actors as well as the children in the audience, and some of the adults, held noisemakers in their hands. The sentries took their positions on the stage, and the rest sat in the chairs provided. Silence fell over the hall as Yome stepped onto the podium and called out: "Mordechai and . . ." He lifted his noisemaker and twirled it around. He was immediately joined by the audience in a deafening ruckus. The name of Haman, who was responsible for the persecution of the Jews in the Book of Esther, could be pronounced only in this way.

Duvid and Shloime positioned themselves at the gate. Duvid leaned against it and Shloime passed through, then he returned shouting, "Jew Mordechai! On your knees when I pass you! By order of the king!"

"I bend my knee only before God, not before any man."

Shloime made an angry, menacing gesture, and both departed.

Now Nuchem sat on the throne, and Shloime knelt before him. "My king, there is a people that lives dispersed and separate among the nations in every province of your realm. They deem themselves better than you, for they ignore your decrees and follow different laws. You would do well to have them destroyed and their possessions added to your treasury."

"These people must be punished!" the king declared. "Send a message to the governors of all 127 satrapies of my realm, from India to Ethiopia. Make known that the Jews are hostile toward everybody, that they have aberrant customs, and in their hatred against us they commit the worst crimes and undermine the stability of the entire empire. I hereby decree that all Jews, including women and children, shall be put to the sword, without mercy or consideration, on the fourteenth day of Adar, so that they will descend into Hades, all together on the same day, and order in the state will remain undisturbed."

Shayndl listened attentively, waiting for her cue. Suddenly she felt touched as never before in all these years. Weren't the Jews of Eastern Europe just as mercilessly exposed to slander and the caprices of those in power? Didn't the book she had just borrowed from Uri describe a similar situation?

"So be it!" Shloime broke with acted triumph into her thoughts.

She was deeply stirred when Duvid stepped onto the stage and leaned against the gate. "Oy, wey is mir," he began his lament. "Esther, my dear, you must do something. He wants to kill us all."

"But who, Uncle Mordechai?"

Duvid twirled his noisemaker and everybody joined in.

"In that case, I would have to see the king," Shayndl replied with pretended fear. "You know that whoever appears before the king unbidden will be put to death, unless the king points his golden scepter at me."

"And the others? Do you want to disown yourself with your silence and become the sole survivor of your people?"

"No, Uncle!" Shayndl stood fully erect. With fiery eyes and firm voice, she declared, "I shall pray and mourn in sackcloth and ashes for three days. Then I shall appear before the king and tell him that I am a Jewess and that . . . ," she twirled her noisemaker briefly, "has slandered us, and if he wants to kill me, so be it."

Sporadic applause encouraged her, and she put all her fervor into the next lines. She took off her cape and stood alone in the center of the stage, dressed only in sackcloth. She raised her hands and gazed at the heavens, reciting the lines she had memorized: "King of all Gods and ruler of the universe, give me strength. You know I despise the crown that has been thrust upon me. Never did I eat at the table of . . . ," she shook the noisemaker, "I drank no sacrificial wine. God, in Your overwhelming mercy, hear the voice of Your people in despair and save us from the hands of our oppressors!" Shayndl was completely carried away—she became the mourning Esther, beseeching God to give her strength.

Rousing applause brought her back to the present. Backstage, in the little room where she changed her clothes, her father greeted her with tears in his eyes. He embraced her and said with a trembling voice, "My child, you were wonderful. The savior of the Jews. That you should be able to act like this shows you're no longer a child." The rare gesture and praise did her heart good. But the last remark felt like a threat. The coming conflict was inescapable.

In the second part of the play, after Esther persuaded the king that she spoke the truth and she saved the Jews, after a huge doll representing Haman had been strung up on the gallows, all the actors assembled onstage. Jubilant, they danced and waved their noisemakers. The audience joined in, and the clapping and twirling could be heard several streets away.

When Shayndl was finally alone, she felt drained. She had dredged up her deepest emotions. And what would her life be like? She could not become a Queen Esther. But she could do something for the cause of justice, something to better the lot of the Jews.

On the way home, Shulim was very attentive. He took Shayndl's hand, and they walked arm in arm through the streets as if they were man and wife. She saw how proud he was of her, and she knew this was the right moment. She took a deep breath and mustered all her courage.

"Papa."

"Yes, my child?"

"Please don't call in the *shadkhen.*"

"But child, why not?" Shulim asked, completely taken by surprise. "Don't you want to get married?"

"Yes, Papa. But I want to choose my own husband."

"But Shayndl, don't you trust your mother and father?"

"Yes. But that is not the point. I want to decide for myself whom I will marry and how I will live."

Shulim stopped walking and shook his head. "What do you mean?" he cried. "We know what is good for you."

They stood facing each other, and Shayndl looked unflinchingly into her father's eyes.

"Papa, please promise you won't force a husband on me."

Her heart was racing, but she knew she had to make it clear to him that she was absolutely serious. "When I meet the man I want to marry, then I'll ask *you* to call in the *shadkhen!*"

"You turn everything upside down," he said. He was completely perplexed.

Shayndl and Avram—1912

Shayndl was floating on a cloud. She wandered down Legionov Boulevard, totally oblivious of what was going on around her. All that existed was the piece of paper she was clutching in her hand. The pedestrians who passed her from the other direction had to dodge quickly out of her way to avoid a collision. Over and over, while she was walking along, she read the Yiddish words in the beloved handwriting.

Oh, that you should sense the passionate fire,
Consuming my proud heart, filled with love's desire.
How sacred your kiss that haunts my dreams of love,
Oh wingèd angel, come ease my heart's distress,
And tear away the walls of loneliness,
Then, soar we shall, like eagles twain, into heaven above.

How bright shines my heart warmed by the sun's gleam,
Frozen once by toil and sorrow's pain.
My dearly belovèd, a rational world will soon arise
On ruins of the old order's just demise,
A world in which no one pawns his soul for bread,
And where liberty and love hold court instead.

Never permit a mask to hide your human countenance,
As I'll always bare mine to you without pretense.
Don't laugh when something makes you cry,
For love means sharing pain and joy.
Never let powdered rouge mask your true intention.
May masks never become our love's affliction.

Only now did she look up, and she asked herself whether she should go to him on the spot. She looked down at her figure. She liked herself in this handmade dress. No, she didn't have to be ashamed to be seen like this. She was quite pleased with her appearance. Yet she discarded the idea. It would not be proper to abandon herself to his embrace so soon after receiving his letter.

Next to the opera house, in the center of the boulevard, was a promenade with benches surrounded by beds of flowers and well-kept lawns. She let a horse-drawn carriage pass, then crossed the roadway and sat down. She read the poem once more, closed her eyes, and let her thoughts wander to the evening when she first saw Avram.

Uri had brought him home. Uri and Mottel had already put their names on the list of prospective emigrants to Palestine, but they were still seeking the family's blessing. Father might take the word of a guest more seriously than their own, they thought. So another chair was pulled up to the table and a plate added.

"This is Avram. He was sentenced to two months in prison in Russia in 1905 for insulting an officer. He came to Austria only a short while ago." Uri introduced his brothers: "Duvid, Avram"— the two namesakes exchanged a grin—"Mottel, and Bezalel." One by one they greeted the guest with a nod. "This is Lemel, the youngest. We are three more. Yisroleh and Golde are married and live elsewhere. And Shayndl will be here any minute."

"How did you insult the officer?" Bezalel wanted to know.

"I refused to step off the sidewalk when he was passing me."

"And for that you're put in jail?" Bezalel asked incredulously.

"If you're a Jew and living in Russia, yes," Avram replied.

"When did this happen?" Shulim asked.

"In 1905."

"Oh, seven years ago. So you fled to this country like many others," Shulim concluded.

"No, I left because I wanted to see the world."

Suddenly the door was flung open and Shayndl rushed in. "I'm sorry, I was held up at Raya's. We were trying to figure out a new pattern. . . ." Dvoire nodded, and Shayndl sat down. She looked at everyone around the table until her eyes came to rest on the guest.

"This is Avram," Uri repeated. "He's from Russia and alone in Lemberg. And this is Shayndl, our youngest sister."

As Avram and Shayndl greeted each other with a smile, Mottel called out, "And Papa's darling." The jealousy in his voice was clearly audible.

Shayndl shot a furious glance at him. The brothers resumed the conversation where it had left off. Questions poured out of them.

"Is it really as bad for Jews in Russia as the Jewish newspapers report? Is it true that Jews are only allowed to live in a confined area of the Ukraine? Are there still that many pogroms?"

Avram made a defensive gesture. "I can't answer everything at once. And besides, I also want to eat," he added, laughing. He nevertheless began to answer their questions and chewed between sentences. "The Jews in Russia have no rights at all. The authorities treat them just as they please."

"Aren't the poor in Russia in the same boat?" asked Duvid.

"Not quite. They certainly live under extremely miserable conditions, but the Jews are despised by everybody, even by the poor. Pogroms still occur, even if they don't come as often as they did after the 1905 Revolution. The Cossacks hound us as if we were wild rabbits."

A shadow suddenly darkened Avram's face. "One of my friends was walking across a field to the neighboring village one day when the Cossacks came riding up behind him. They stopped him and pulled down his pants. When they saw he was circumcised, they simply slit his throat. In the nearest inn, they boasted that they had again avenged the murder of Christ. Peasants found the body and took it to his parents."

Shayndl was horrified. Shulim, too, turned pale. He said, "Since we have come under Austrian rule, nothing of the sort happens here anymore."

"Anti-Semitism here is not as open and brutal as in Russia, Papa," Uri said, "but the Poles have just as little love for us."

"Yes, you're right," Shulim conceded, "but they let us live, and we should be grateful for that."

"Grateful? For what?" Uri clenched his fist under the table. Mottel, too, was getting riled up.

"Papa! You sound just like the assimilationists with your gratitude! What wouldn't they give to be real Poles? Papa! Only in our own Jewish state . . ."

Dvoire cut him off. "Mottel, you hothead! Don't you dare yell at your father like that!"

Uri looked at Avram. Would he say something? The twenty-nine-year-old man spoke in a conciliatory tone. "Well, you know,

Mottel, these assimilationists, as you call them so scornfully, are right in some respects. We have to adapt to modern life. Whether a Jewish state in Palestine is the solution, though, I find very questionable."

Uri looked at his guest aghast and disappointed, especially since he knew him from Poale Zion.

"But how else can we protect ourselves?" Shayndl interjected. She repeated the story of Nuchem Friedmann and the razor-blade gang.

Avram nodded. He had heard many such stories. He said, "One condition for solving these problems is the abolition of poverty." It was obvious that he had expressed this idea many times. "And that is only possible if the wealth is distributed more equitably. When everybody has enough, then it won't be so easy to incite people against each other. Three-quarters of the people living in the great czarist empire are illiterate; they can neither read nor write. Very few can afford to send children to school there. But if people were better educated, then they would not turn such a willing ear to the priests' stories about us being descended from the devil."

"From the devil!" Dvoire screamed with fright at the word being mentioned. "May no evil eye meet us!"

"In Germany, many of the best-known doctors, lawyers, writers, and artists are Jews," Avram continued.

Uri objected. "But you said yourself, Avram, that they have almost forgotten that they're Jews."

"And in the hundred years since they were granted citizens' rights, they have also learned to lick the boots of the goyim," Duvid added scornfully.

Now Bezalel spoke up. "Many Jewish fathers don't even like to see their sons attend the four years of obligatory schooling here because there is less time left for studying the sacred writings." He blinked at his father, who kept silent.

"We don't need to leave the country to study," Avram said, turning toward Uri. "If all Jews were simply to leave, the problem would just be shifted to Palestine. What we need is a fundamental change in the social situation so that there would be no rich, no poor, no factory owners . . ."

"I presume you get your pearls of wisdom from one of those

workers' circles," Shulim cut in, speaking in a soft but sarcastically icy tone.

Avram nodded.

"You're an assimilationist, just of the socialist sort!" Mottel called reproachfully across the table, pointing his finger at Avram. His tea glass tipped over; the tablecloth turned brown.

Dvoire said, "All right, big mouth, you can use big words, but can you also fetch a rag?" Mottel looked at her embarrassed and quickly left the room.

"Avram, maybe you're right," said Uri. "When nobody has too little, then nobody will have too much, either. But we remain Jews, whether we like it or not. The others make sure of that."

Mottel came back with a kitchen rag, with which he patted the tablecloth.

"Oh, give it to me," Shayndl said impatiently, and took over.

"We were always the outcasts, the strangers," Shulim proclaimed. "We speak a different language, we have a different God, different customs and values. And for this we must be grateful. For we don't kill people out of hatred, we don't oppress others. No Jew gets senselessly drunk like so many of the goyim do every day. At most we drink on our holidays, but even then not to excess. When the others use violence to tear us away from God, they merely prove that they are the barbarians. A Jew who does not observe our laws betrays himself and all of us. His body and soul are poisoned, life loses its purpose, and he might as well go and hang himself."

"And sometimes I think that would be best," Dvoire said wearily into the tense silence. Two red spots appeared on Shulim's face, his eyes flashed with anger. He turned not only his head but his whole body toward his wife.

"Dvoire!" he shouted. "You have no right to even think such a thing, let alone wish it!" Shayndl, too, was startled. Rarely had she seen her father in such a state of agitation. "Do you want everything to have been for nothing? We survived the centuries! Despite them! Their slanders, their humiliations, even their massacres were unable to destroy us. We, all of us, sitting here," he looked at each face, "have the duty"—his fist came crashing down on the table— "to survive!"

And if we wait here until the Moshiach comes, we'll be wiped out in the meantime, Uri thought, looking at Shayndl. She nodded at him as if he had spoken aloud. Shulim slumped back into his chair.

Soon after that evening, Shayndl happened to meet Avram in the street. She had admired the firmness with which he had stood up to her father. He is no weather vane turning with the wind, she thought. He cares for others, he thinks about the ways of the world and fights for justice. Just as I would like to do. She looked into his face as they greeted each other. He is certainly good-looking, she noted, and was flattered when he invited her, just a teenager, to join him at a coffeehouse.

Lemberg, known as the second Vienna and the pearl of Galicia, had many small, reasonably priced coffeehouses, where one could sit for a long time reading or chatting without being disturbed. Shayndl felt very grown up when Avram held the door for her, steered her by the elbow toward an empty table, and held the chair for her.

Avram wondered how he could best impress her and decided to take the direct approach. "Do you know that you're a very beautiful girl?" Shayndl blushed and demurely shook her head. "Yes, you are. You should know this and be proud."

"Thank you," she said embarrassedly, and quickly changed the subject.

"Why did you leave Russia?" she asked, using the formal address.

"Why don't you say *du* to me?" She nodded in agreement. "Didn't I tell the story when I was at your place? Oh yes, you came in late," he remembered. Now he saw no harm in padding the truth a bit.

"I was a member of a student group in Kiev that planned to assassinate the czar. Unfortunately, the attempt failed, and I was banished for three years to Siberia. I was able to escape and fled across the border in women's clothes."

Shayndl's eyes widened. She had heard of such heroes and was now very flattered to be sitting in a coffeehouse with one who gave her his undivided attention.

In the weeks that followed, Avram called at her parents' home with increasing frequency. Shayndl was always present when he told this or that story about his life. With the exception of Shulim, the

whole family clung to his every word. With wit and color, he paint-
ed a world at once familiar and strange—familiar, because it was a
Jewish world, and strange, because it was filled with adventure and
rebellion, making their own lives appear drab and unexciting. He
frequently made the whole family laugh, and he quite obviously rel-
ished his role as an entertainer. Everyone joined in when, with his
lovely voice and fiery eyes, he launched into songs exhorting the
downtrodden to fight against injustice. But he also sang Yiddish
love songs that warmed Shayndl's heart. With every visit, she was
drawn to him more. Once she even fell into stammering when he
spoke to her.

Some time after that, Uri suggested that Shayndl go to the Yiddish theater with him, and, as though by coincidence, Avram joined
them. From then on he invited her regularly to the coffeehouse.
They flirted, laughed, and had serious conversations in which they
exchanged ideas. For Avram, a stranger in this city, she was like an
angel who relieved his loneliness and bewitched him with her spon-
taneity and eagerness to learn. She wanted to know everything he
had to tell. And in turn, she had never enjoyed so much attention
from a mature man. Rarely had she laughed so much as in his company. She told him of the promise she had wrung from her father.
"He has left me alone now for the last two years, but the thought
that he will soon try to force a husband on me hangs over me like a
death sentence."

"He is a fanatic," Avram said. "He has lived his life for the traditions and is incapable of seeing that the changes going on in the
world are progress. I can understand him. Because people like your
father have never been able to sink their roots into the earth, they
were forced to push them upward into heaven. And he cannot
imagine a different life for his children." Shayndl nodded, troubled,
but she felt warm and sheltered by his wisdom and concern.

Despite the fact that her parents tolerated his visits—since one
did not close the door to a stranger, but shared food and warmth
with him—Shayndl was not oblivious to their misgivings. Once,
when she expressed her enthusiasm for the guest, Shulim said, "Yes,
he is very colorful, but it is all a sham. He is unreliable and has no
depth. Besides, a man like that calls himself a Jew? Not even on
Rosh Hashanah and Yom Kippur does he go to shul. He's nothing
but a rootless adventurer."

Shayndl remained silent. With Avram, she thought, she would not have to keep a kosher household. He would never force her to wear only long sleeves and dresses buttoned up to the neck, let alone hide her hair under a wig as Jewish law demands of a married woman. As his wife, she would not have to have one child after another.

Now Shayndl held the poem in her hand. It told her he needed her and he loved her. When he called at the house that evening, he gave her a quizzical look. Her shy, furtive glance was his answer; no word was spoken. She showed him to the door when he was leaving. He whispered, "Will you come to me tomorrow at seven?" She nodded and hurried away.

That night she was unable to sleep, so filled was she with hopes and longing. She wrapped her arms around her body and dreamed they were his. She buried her face in her pillow and imagined it was his neck. She could almost feel his kiss. At last she was overcome by tiredness and fell into a restless sleep.

The next day at supper, she was the first to leave the table. A few minutes before seven, she was in front of Avram's door. He opened the door, pulled her inside, and kissed her in a long, passionate embrace until she gasped for air. When she turned her mouth away, he let go of her, and they entered the room together. It was the first of many visits, during the course of which he read her his own poems, they sang together, and they continued the conversations they had begun in the coffeehouses. Frequently the room echoed with their laughter. He not only had a good sense of humor; he was also a storyteller who could depict an ordinary situation with irony and keen observation, which was amusing and provided a fresh perspective.

When Avram visited the family, they acted as if nothing had happened between them. However, during the twelve months they knew each other, a decisive event took place, at least for the by-then-seventeen-year-old Shayndl. Avram said to her one day, "Shayndl, my love, you must trust me. I will now make you a woman, and then I'll be your man. Just close your eyes and put yourself into my hands."

❁

I Am Somebody!—Who Am I?

O nce we were slaves of Pharaoh in Egypt when God led us out from there. Had the Holy One, blessed be He, not taken our ancestors out of Egypt, then we, our children, and all our descendants would still be slaves of the pharaohs. Therefore, it is our duty to tell the story of the exodus from Egypt to our children and their children, and everyone who speaks about it in great detail is to be praised . . ."

It was Pesach; the whole family sat around the festively decked-out table. Every nook and cranny of the small apartment had been cleaned so that not even the minutest crumb of leavened bread was left in the house. The crockery had been scalded in a huge kettle, because they could not afford three separate sets of dishes: one for *milkhiges*, one for *fleishiges,* and one for Pesach, as was common among the well-to-do. Dvoire had worked very hard. She took great care to make sure that not a speck of *hametz* or dirt was left, not even a faint trace of milkfat in a cup from which someone might drink meat broth later on.

Shayndl, too, was exhausted. She sat next to Avram as though by coincidence. Uri had made sure that Avram would be invited, and their parents had agreed, for one of the prayers on the Seder evening says: "Whoever is hungry, let him come and eat with us; whoever is needy, let him come and celebrate Passover with us. This year here, next year in Jerusalem; this year slaves, next year free men. Amen."

The contented sounds of slurping and smacking were interspersed with chatter and the chanting of prayers. The wine had made them quite merry. That evening all conflicts were pushed aside. The bonds between them gave each strength and security that was to be found only in a family. They all felt this. Shayndl, too. Under the table, she stroked Avram's hand.

The table was cleared and the dirty dishes put away. Everybody leaned back comfortably and they sang together:

Then came the Eternal, blessed be He,
and punished the *malach hamuves* [angel of death],
who killed the *shoichet* [butcher],
who slaughtered the ox,
who drank the water,
that put out the fire,
that burned the stick,
that beat the dog,
that bit the cat,
that ate the lamb,
that my father bought for two *zuzim*
chad gadya, chad gadya . . .

They were all in an exuberant mood when Shulim suddenly sat up straight and proclaimed: "I have an announcement to make. Good news. I would have liked to have seen Shayndl married last year, but she asked me to wait. Now that she is seventeen, I have called the *shadkhen*. In two weeks he will visit us with the groom and his family."

Something snapped in Shayndl's head. She felt as though she were being run over by a steamroller and ground into the earth. She stared at her father with wide-open eyes. Her scream tore into the tense silence that had fallen over the company. "Papa! You can't do this to me! Papa! I've found the man I want to marry." She felt so miserable, she wanted to crawl under the table and disappear into a hole. Her gaze fell on Avram, and she was grateful for his encouraging look.

"Tell him," he said softly.

"Avram and I want to get married, Papa!"

Shulim froze. His gentle, cheerful, charming, beautiful Shayndl! How could she slap him in the face like this? Of all people, she had to fall for this adventurer who did not take the traditions, no, who took nothing at all, seriously, whose children will grow up as heathens. And she wants to throw herself away on such a rake! He rose. Into the crackling silence that hung over the room, his voice resounded like divine thunder: "Mr. Genin! Please leave my house and don't *ever come back again!*" He punctuated the last four words with slow, heavy emphasis. Avram got up from his chair and left.

Shulim held on to the table to steady himself. He suddenly felt a sharp pain in his heart, as if his own beloved daughter had pierced it with a knife. It was precisely because she was his one and only that he had given in again and again to her wishes. He had tried to raise her with kindness, to make a pious Jewess of her. Now he regretted his indulgence. *I should have locked her up.*

Deeply shaken, Shayndl thought, he disrespects me and does not even notice it. She looked at her mother, so haggard and always overworked. She did not know whether she should scream in anger or cry with pity. Whenever I needed you, you never had an ear for me, she thought. Shayndl said not another word on this Seder night of Pesach 1913.

"I slept with him." Shayndl looked her parents straight in the eye. They stood stiff, paralyzed, before her. A whistle was heard in the yard. For weeks, this had been Avram's signal.

"And now I have to go. You refuse to let Avram come here, so he is waiting for me downstairs. Papa, I am going to marry Avram whether you like it or not."

Shulim left the kitchen, slamming the door behind him. The echo was still reverberating in the air when Dvoire said softly and beseechingly to her daughter, "He'll make you unhappy, my child. He is not the kind of man you can tie down in a marriage. He will take his liberties, also at your expense. As soon as you have children, he will leave you."

Shayndl shook her head. "No. He will make me happy, Mama."

For months Shulim was unable to come to grips with the fact that his *teybele,* his little dove, his own flesh and blood, had abandoned God and had given herself to such a good-for-nothing. Whenever he heard the shrill whistling, he cringed as if he had been stabbed with a knife. He began to avoid Shayndl's presence altogether so he would not have to see her slipping quickly into her coat and out the door. She showed no shame at all about defying him this way! A tense air hung now permanently over the apartment, and the topic was consciously avoided. Dvoire felt helplessly caught between her husband and her daughter, and was powerless to mediate.

Shayndl, too, cried herself to sleep for a long time after the quarrel. Who was she without her father's blessing? Yet she simply could not obey and submit to his will. In the apartment they passed each other in silence, fought to suppress their own pain, did not see that of the other. The more time passed, the more their hearts hardened against each other.

The outbreak of the Great War—only after the Second World War had begun did it occur to anyone that this was the first—caused new problems for Shayndl. Austria and Germany fought against France, Great Britain, and Russia. As long as victories on the battlefield were being celebrated, nobody paid much attention to any Russian citizens who might be living in Austria. When defeat became an ominous possibility, the foreigners were interned.

Shayndl in 1916.

In the spring of 1916, when Shayndl knocked on Avram's door, she received no answer. A neighbor told her, "He was picked up yesterday. All Russians are being taken away. Didn't you know?"

Shayndl had to hold on to the handrail to keep from being overcome by a spell of nausea. This had happened several times in the last few weeks. At first she had been puzzled. When her period did not come, she understood. What would Avram say? Would he want the child? She was relieved when he took the news with a happy smile. "Well, then we'll just have to get married," he had said.

Now Shayndl stood in the stairwell. She knew she had to be married to Avram before the child was born. First she had to find out where he was. Of all places, they had taken him to a prison in

Budapest. She explained her situation to the official and told him that she must be married before October when the baby was due. The broad grin on his face made her blush a bright red. She would have liked nothing better than to run from the room in a fit of tears. But she overcame her embarrassment and insisted on her request. The official consulted with his superior. When he came back, he told her, "Permission has been granted for you to marry the prisoner Avram Genin at the prison in Budapest. Then he can leave the prison and settle in a small town near Budapest, where his activities can be monitored, until the war is over. Then he will be released."

She breathed a sigh of relief. The first hurdle was taken.

"Hello, Shayndl! How come you are visiting me here?" asked Dvoire, glad to see her daughter enter the shop.

"Mama, I'm pregnant. Avram is interned in a prison in Budapest. I'm going to him." She spoke the words in a hard, defiant tone.

"When?" Dvoire asked softly. Her face was pale.

"The child? It's due in October. I'm leaving as soon as I can get the money together for the train fare."

Dvoire sank down on the chair behind the counter. She lifted her eyes upward: "Why, dear God, why do you see fit to punish me this way?" Then looking at Shayndl, "I don't know what Papa will do."

When Shayndl came home that evening she found her father in the living room, sitting erect and motionless as if he had swallowed a stick. He said with bitterness, "The sooner you leave, the better."

A week before the planned departure, Dvoire asked Shayndl to come see her at the shop. With calm practicality, she handed her daughter four towels, some linen, a set of tableware, and baby clothing. "This is your trousseau. The baby things are from a customer. Her baby has outgrown them."

She embraced her daughter in a rare impulsive gesture and wiped away the tears. They faced each other, for the first time not as mother and daughter, but as two women who understood more about each other than any man in those days was willing to know.

"I hope and pray that you will find happiness and that you made the right decision. Don't mention anything about these things to Papa. He needn't know."

Shayndl, too, was fighting back the tears. "Thank you," she said, and meant it not only for the parcel she had just received. It was a relief to know her mother was on her side. She left the shop in a lighter mood than she had entered it, despite the heavy package she was carrying.

At the end of August 1916, Shayndl stood next to her packed suitcase in the corridor of her parents' apartment. She wore a new hat and a dress made to conceal her swelling belly. Uri, Mottel, and Bezalel, waiting to take her to the station, urged her to hurry. She went back one more time into the living room to say good-bye to her parents.

"Papa, I'm going now. Please give me your blessing."

He rose from his chair and looked at her with cold eyes. When she tried to embrace him, he pushed her away. "Be well," he said, and extended his hand as if to a stranger.

Dvoire wept. She embraced her daughter and wished her "mazel tov." Shayndl left the room in a somber mood, but the sight of her brothers, who pulled her away with "Come on, we have to go or you'll miss the train," made her forget her father's coldness. A little while later, the train pulled out of the station, and she let herself fall back into the seat. Calm, collected, and full of hope, she looked forward to being reunited with Avram.

Shayndl was still full of courage and determination when she was seated in a chair facing the prison director's desk. Her hands were folded over her belly, and she could feel the baby kicking inside. In his singsong Viennese, the director promised to call a rabbi who would marry them in the prison.

Two days later, after the ceremony, sitting on the bed in a run-down hotel room, she finally broke down. This was not the kind of wedding a young girl dreams about. No canopy under which the bride and the groom meet, no wineglass that he smashes under his heels, no admiring or envious glances, no well-wishing from friends and relatives, no party with several hundred dancing guests . . . This blushing bride had no reason to blush. She had to muster all her strength during the ceremony to keep up her resolve. Now that she had reached her goal, the years of tension, of strife, and the terrible silence at home took their toll. A flood of tears burst out of her.

"Control yourself!" she scolded herself amidst the sobbing, only to break down all the more. The tears brought some relief, but she could not forgive herself for her weakness. She did not remember when it was that she had learned to be ashamed of her tears. She did not remember how often she, a small child not yet able to speak, had cried in a corner of the crowded apartment without anybody paying attention to her. Only when her cries became angry and turned into insistent screams did Dvoire put down her work and send one of Shayndl's brothers to see what was the matter. If the reason was immediately apparent, then the matter was taken care of; if not, then she heard angry accusations of "You just want to be pampered! Be quiet!"

Still in tears, she suddenly saw herself as a two-year-old, climbing onto Avram's knees and leaning her head, sobbing, against his broad chest. She could almost feel his hand gently stroking her head, the way her father often used to do. The vision eased her pain, and she stopped crying. "He's your husband now," she told herself. "Soon he'll be released from prison, and then we'll live together." A comforting feeling rushed through her. They would then merge together, and she would dissolve herself completely in him. He would wipe away all pain and make her happy. That was, after all, what a husband was there for. But what if her parents had been right? She pushed that thought far, far from her mind.

Married

The authorities kept their word. Before long, Avram was released from prison and allowed to settle in a small town near Budapest. He was given a job, and Shayndl was able to join him. Stretched out in their bed that night, she looked around. The rented room was bright and nicely furnished. It is not a bad place in which to live out the war. Certainly not as crowded as at home, she thought. She nestled against Avram and was happy. Shayndl enjoyed the love of this mature man and the intimacy between them, and she was quite sure that it would never end.

As always when she was lying down, she could feel the child move inside her. She took Avram's hand and placed it gently on her large belly so that he, too, could feel it. She beamed at him in the dark and tenderly stroked his face. "My dear Shayndl, my dear little fighter," he whispered into her ear, his hand caressing her naked body. She clung to him and knew that the fight had been worthwhile.

Rebecca, named after Avram's mother, Rifka, was born in October 1916. Her parents were very happy.

Avram worked at a printer's shop, and Shayndl tended to the household and the child. But although the child occupied much of her time, an unexpected feeling of emptiness she was unable to overcome or even explain began to creep into her life. Their relationship had lost the exhilaration and tension of the forbidden. And even though she enjoyed the luxury of a room for only the three of them, something was missing. Her time and thoughts had always been filled with other people; now she was suddenly left to herself, and she did not know what to do with her time or herself. You have no reason to be dissatisfied, she told herself again and again. On the contrary! After all, you got what you fought for. Be reasonable, she said to herself, but she really meant, don't be so weak! She stood in front of the mirror, smoothed her hair, and smiled helplessly: "I am doing well. I am happy." And she waited longingly for the evening and for Avram.

However, there were days when Avram made her feel very insecure. In Lemberg, when they were together, he had always been the
strong one. She had put herself into his hands, ready to subordinate
her will to his. Now, he sometimes came home from work, gave her
a cursory kiss on the forehead, sat down and silently begin to eat
the lovingly prepared cheese-filled pierogi or whatever else she had
cooked.

"Avram," she asked apprehensively, "are you angry with me?"

"No, why?" he replied, surprised.

"You're so distant."

Impatiently, he answered, "Shayndl, I'm tired, that's all. I just
can't be social right now."

"Well," she said, "then I'll tell you something." Deeply relieved,
she plunged into an account of her day. "Just imagine, at the mar-
ket, I was able to bargain the vegetable vendor down by a third
because Rebecca started to scream so loud, the woman was glad to
get rid of us."

She had hoped that this little story would amuse him and that he
would praise her shrewdness. Instead, he listened indulgently,
almost with a pained face, to her chatter. Her daily routine did not
interest him, and he never spoke about his, as if it were of no concern to her. Why did he shut her out of his life? She fell silent, and
he seemed relieved by it.

He could not talk to her about the awful secret he was trying to
hide. If she knew, she would certainly turn away from me, he
thought. Even while still in prison, he had noticed the rash that
caused him so much anguish. He knew where it came from. The
prison cell to which he was confined was already occupied by three
men when he arrived. He had barely fallen asleep the first night
when he was brutally woken up. A hand pressed against his mouth
muffled his scream, strong arms pinned him down so he could not
move. With a jerk he was flipped on his stomach and tied to the
bed with a sheet, and . . . He tried to wipe out the memory, but it
rose again and again, accompanied by a feeling of disgust mixed
with sexual excitement. They had raped him, all three had raped
him. What was left was fear and shame.

Shortly after he and Shayndl had arrived in the little town, he
consulted a doctor without telling Shayndl. The diagnosis was

quickly made: syphilis! This terrible, lingering disease, which frequently led to death! He kept his horror locked inside. It often happened that he did not feel well after his visits to the doctor. Then Shayndl's mere presence made him irritable.

He sighed. He would have liked nothing better than to let himself go and to nestle up against her like a little boy. But he knew she expected him to be strong and he did not want to disappoint her. In bed that evening, he put his arms around her. She clung to him like a hurt child that needed comforting. He stroked her face and kissed away her tears. They slept next to each other, each alone with his fears.

One day a letter came from Uri.

Dear Shayndl,

I was very happy to receive your telegram. Congratulations! May Rebecca bring you much joy. I am sorry I did not write sooner, but something terrible has happened here. Until now, I have not had the courage to tell you about it. But you must know.

After you were gone, Papa sat in his chair for days without saying a word. He only left the house for the morning and evening prayers. It was as if he were nursing a deep wound. Then he sat shiva for you. I still cannot believe it. He declared you dead! He did not shed a single tear. Mama all the more. We are not allowed to speak your name in the house.

Shayndl, I am going away now. My next letter to you will probably come from Palestine. I don't want to speak with Papa anymore. He carried on as if his dearly beloved wife had run off with another man. You should know that I find the whole affair reprehensible. My dear Shayndl, be assured that I will always help you if I can. I admire you very much. You have the courage to go your own way, and that is important if one wants to remain human. Stay the way you are.

I wish you all the happiness you have hoped for.

Affectionately, your brother,
Uri

Shayndl tried in vain to control the spasm that tore her stomach. She dragged herself from the chair to the bed and let herself collapse. She lay there with eyes closed as if she were unconscious.

Almost without breathing, she turned on her side and rolled herself up like a baby inside its mother. Out of the blackness before her eyes emerged a deformed, two-headed monster. It had short little stick legs and long heavy arms. One of its faces was twisted with pain and fear; the other was defiant and spewing hatred. Both heads were covered with the thick, wavy hair Shayndl had in common with her father. She saw the monster cowering in front of a tall knight in shining armor who was surrounded by a beautiful light. In his raised hands, the knight held an ax with which he was about to split the deformed body in two. As the ax descended, Shayndl shook herself out of the nightmare. Yes, she thought, to be dead now, that would be for the best. Her child's cries brought her back to the present.

Avram came home and read the letter. "Don't worry about it, Shayndl. Your father will never understand us." His words were meant to comfort her, but she was already beyond his reach. She had become the ugly, two-headed monster that had masked itself with the beautiful hair. Silently, they sat down to supper. Again, each remained alone with his own fears.

✿

Kraków

The end of the war brought in its wake the collapse of the Austro-Hungarian Empire. When Shayndl traveled from Lemberg to Budapest in 1916, she did not have to cross a single border. In 1918, when she and Avram left the little town near Budapest for Kraków, they traveled from Hungary to Poland. Shayndl and Avram settled with their daughter in the Polish city of Kraków. They rented a room and bought secondhand furniture. With the move to a new town, they seemed to have left all their fears behind them. Avram found work as a printer, the most prestigious trade among the working classes. He knew five languages to a greater or lesser degree of perfection: Russian, Polish, German, Hebrew, and, of course, Yiddish. Shayndl's expectations of being cared for and made happy were finally being fulfilled. She still wanted to do something great for mankind, but she did not know how and where. So she contented herself with the next best thing: her child and household. She met other young women with children at the playground or while shopping, and they visited each other. Sometimes Shayndl and Avram would go to the theater or the cinema, and at night she lay contentedly in his arms, basking in his passionate embrace.

When Avram went to work in the morning, he looked forward all day to the warmth and affection that awaited him on his return home. Now and then he brought friends with him. Then there were interesting discussions at the dinner table. Avram particularly looked forward to holding Shayndl in his arms at night. He had made her a woman and she had become a wonderful one. In those first years in Kraków, they felt little of that from which both suffered: the inability to love.

The idyll did not last. Avram became increasingly restless. After all, he had left Russia to see the world. You sure have come far, he said to himself. He became increasingly moody and impatient, especially with his little daughter. If she did not react quickly enough, he would say, "You're a real blockhead. You'll never amount to anything."

Shayndl often felt rejected and abused by his ill temper. She noticed that sometimes she was glad when Avram came home late, but she still reproached him bitterly for doing so. For him, the family was becoming a stone around his neck. So both withdrew into themselves and barely knew what to do with each other. They never spoke about what touched them most deeply. As before, Shayndl did not know what Avram did outside the house, and he never asked her what she did all day. During the six years they lived in Kraków, their nights together increasingly became for Shayndl an opportunity to extract some tenderness from her husband; for Avram they were a duty he expected of her. She submitted to his every wish, not only because he was the ax-wielding knight, but also because she still hoped that one day their fading love would blossom again.

In November 1924, a second daughter, Malka, was born. Shortly afterward, in the early morning hours of a January day in 1925, Shayndl was in for a big shock. A loud, hard knock on the door roused them from their sleep. Startled, they sat up. Shayndl slipped out of bed and went to the door.

"Who is it?" she called through the closed door in Polish.

"The police!"

She gave Avram an apprehensive look. "What do you want from us?" she asked through the door. Avram was sitting up straight in bed, white as a sheet.

"Avram Genin lives here, doesn't he?" said a man's voice. Shayndl unlocked the door with trembling hands. Two Polish policemen in uniform stormed past her and positioned themselves menacingly in front of Avram. "Get dressed! You're under arrest!" one of them barked.

Shayndl pulled at the man's sleeve and asked, flustered and indignant, "What is he supposed to have done? Do you have a warrant for his arrest? You can't just burst in here like this!"

The policeman grinned at her. "Believe me, I don't get up this early in the morning for the fun of it," he said, pulling a piece of paper from his pocket and holding it close to her face.

Shayndl quickly skimmed the Polish words. It really was an arrest warrant. What does it say? For counterfeiting? She looked at Avram, who was slowly pulling on his pants with downcast eyes, carefully avoiding hers.

"Avram, is this true? You have been involved in counterfeiting?" His silence was answer enough.

The policeman eyed Shayndl more closely. He did not understand the Yiddish words, but he guessed their meaning from the exchange of glances.

"You don't seem to know that your husband is a member of a whole gang of counterfeiters," he said, pocketing the arrest warrant. "He's a good printer, he knows his trade," he said sarcastically.

Shayndl could only shake her head. She felt her way backward toward the bed and let herself fall, staring into space until the door fell shut and they were gone. Only then did she give herself over to despair. The hero she had married, the fighter for justice and a better future for the human race, had turned out to be a common criminal, a lowlife, an ordinary counterfeiter.

"A con man, that's what he is!" she screamed furiously over and over, pulling her hair. Malka started to cry and Rebecca stared, frightened, at her mother.

Shayndl just could not believe it. Had he been arrested for political reasons, she would have been able to bear it. She would have tried to carry on with her head held high, for his sake and for the sake of the good cause. But her husband a criminal? She was deeply ashamed. What would become of them now?

Avram was sentenced to three years in prison, and she knew she had to pull through all by herself. But how? She did not know how to support herself, let alone two children. In the first few months, she sold the furniture, piece by piece. Although she knew better, she had the feeling that Avram had abandoned her. After all, ugly monster that she was, she did not deserve anything else. She could not admit to herself that she wanted to stop living, for at home she had learned that no one had a right to throw life away, that survival was the ultimate duty, no matter what the cost. And she knew the children needed her. She had to force herself to get out of bed every morning and to carry on.

She found work as a steam presser in a Jewish textile factory. But what should she do with the children? Rebecca was taken in by the family of one of the accomplices. "To ease their conscience," Shayndl said bitterly. "Avram had to bear the brunt of the punishment for the others. They all escaped to Holland in time without giving him a warning!"

During the first winter, there was not enough money to buy fuel, so Rebecca was permitted to take home as much coal as she could carry. In return, the family treated her like a maid who had to earn her keep.

Malka was five months old when Shayndl put her in the care of the nuns at a Catholic convent. This went totally against her grain. To her it was as if she were going to her enemies for help. But what else could she do? Her pride did not allow her to turn to her parents. Soon Shayndl noticed that Malka was not getting enough to eat. And on top of everything, the child came down with scarlet fever. Shayndl bitterly reproached the nuns. "I guess a Jewish brat doesn't need a decent meal or proper care!" After work and on weekends, she went to the convent to make sure her child was kept alive. Malka remained with the nuns all of six months, until Shayndl was able to afford to pay somebody to take care of her.

With time Shayndl settled into her new, daily routine: up early in the morning, eight hours or more standing on her feet at the ironing board, returning home and bathing her poor, tired feet, supper for herself and her two daughters, then falling dead tired into bed.

She visited Avram regularly in prison. During most of the visiting time she rebuked him bitterly. But when she was told one day that he was no longer there, that he had been deported to where he came from, she was deeply distressed. To Soviet Russia? Should she follow him? She was relieved to hear a short while later that the Soviet authorities had decided they had plenty of thieves of their own. Avram was deprived of his citizenship and sent back to Poland. As a result, he was now stateless, and the same went for his wife and children. This did not bother Shayndl. She had always felt unwanted in Poland, anyway.

Although she was often tired, in these three years she began to appreciate her new independence. She felt surprisingly strong. She had made decisions that had turned out to be right. She had proved herself capable of providing for herself and the children. Now and then she even managed to bring a few delicacies for Avram in prison. These were the kind of accomplishments nobody thought a woman capable of, and it gave her a new sense of self-confidence. But she had also found help along the way. Her landlady, Mrs.

Farsztendik, permitted her to live in the rented room for three whole years completely rent free. For this she was still grateful decades later.

But what did the future hold for her? Would she ever be able to trust Avram again? She would have to try. Living without him, without a man, was unthinkable for her. From early childhood, she had learned that a woman without a man was like a fish without water. Besides, he was the father of her children and had been her first and only lover.

The three years passed. On the day of Avram's release, she and the children put on their best clothes and went to pick him up at prison. A somewhat haggard but still strong man in a worn, now old-fashioned suit met them. Rebecca recognized him right away and rushed toward him. He caught her in his arms and twirled her round and round. Shayndl held Malka, who looked apprehensively at the stranger.

"Malka, this is your Papa. He will be staying with us from now on." Avram reached for her, but the almost-four-year-old clung to her mother and started to cry.

"Let her be," said Shayndl.

Avram nodded. "She'll get used to me."

In the streetcar that took them home, they sat together once again as a family: Rebecca between her parents and Malka on her mother's lap. Shayndl was deeply relieved. Independence may be all right, but her greatest longing was for a normal family life. Now they could enjoy it once again.

At home, she showed off the new furniture. Then followed a delicious meal: borscht from red beets with hot potatoes, then gefilte fish, followed by baked chicken, and applesauce for dessert. Avram leaned back, satisfied. "Shayndl, my love, for three years I have longed for your good cooking."

She pulled her chair close to his and leaned against his shoulder. "With a police record, it will be hard for you to find work, Avram."

He nodded. "We're stateless, we're Jews. I'm thinking of emigrating," he said hesitantly.

Shayndl's face lit up. She, too, had been thinking along those lines. She said, "You know, Uri is now in Brazil. Bezalel first joined

Mottel in Palestine and now he is in Australia. Many Jews here have left for America. Why don't we go too? I would so much like to live in a civilized country."

Avram looked at his wife with growing attentiveness. She was no longer the child he had married. She had thought about things and was able to make suggestions. "Seems you asked around," he said.

"What else should I do, on my own with the children!" He ignored the reproach, and she continued to dream aloud about the possibilities that were open to them in the United States. But how were they to get there without money?

"Let's go to Berlin first," Shayndl suggested. "One can make a good living there—at least until we've saved enough for the ship's passage. The Germans are hardworking, thorough, and very disciplined. I read in a magazine that German products are in high demand all over the world."

She saw how her knowledge impressed him. "And they don't have any anti-Semitic laws. The Jews in Germany have been equal citizens for a long time."

Avram leaned back, unable to suppress a smile at his wife's long speech, but he said nothing.

"Well," she sighed, "we don't have to stay there for long. But it will take a good two to three years before we'll have saved up enough. Meanwhile, the children could learn something of the cleanliness and order that is lacking here." She remembered a saying she liked very much: "It is, after all, a civilized country of thinkers and poets, whereas here we live among barbarians."

When Shayndl and Avram decided to emigrate to the United States via Berlin, they had no idea how little critical thinking, let alone poetry writing, was being done there. Not in their wildest dreams could they have imagined that the world-renowned German virtues of discipline and order would bring forth a blind obedience, which, coupled with hard work and thoroughness, would, almost fifteen years later, murder almost all of their relatives who were then still living in Europe.

They decided that Avram would go ahead first. He would look for work and rent a place for them to live. Then, when he was settled, he would write and have Shayndl and the children follow. She and the two girls saw him off at the train station. They stood on the platform and waved until the train disappeared into the far distance.

❈

Berlin—The Metropolis

Shayndl waited for a letter from Avram. Day after day passed, but none came. At the end of three weeks, she resolutely sold all her belongings. This yielded just enough for one one-way train ticket to Berlin. Malka was still small and did not need a ticket. But what about Rebecca, who was already twelve years old?

Before they boarded the train, Shayndl gave her older daughter strict instructions. The ride to Berlin would take twelve hours. Rebecca was to take a seat in a different compartment, and when the conductor came around to check the tickets, she should pretend to be sleeping. Shayndl and Malka would be in the next car. Rebecca understood that she really had to be on her toes or they might get thrown off the train at any station along the way. How would they then make it without money and in a strange place?

When they arrived without incident at the Schlesische Bahnhof in Berlin, they were tired but greatly relieved. Shayndl looked around at the confusion of platforms, at the people greeting and embracing each other. Shouts and whistles droned in her ears. Would she ever find her way in this big city? She dragged her only suitcase along the platform, holding onto Malka with one hand and relying on Rebecca not to lose sight of her in the crowd. How would she find the Jewish community center? Should she just ask somebody? In Poland she would not have dared to do so. But this was Germany, and she was sure she could risk it.

She sat her children down on a bench and waited until the crowd had dispersed somewhat. Then she approached the man at the information booth with her question. The railroad official knew the answer. How many exhausted, hunted, bedraggled human beings had he seen getting off the train in recent years who had asked him the same question? Countless. Since he felt pity for them, he had inquired about it so he could give them the right information.

"You must go the Jewish Welfare Agency, young lady. That's at Rosenstrasse 3. Go up these stairs," he pointed at the staircase, "then turn left and go up one more flight, the one with the sign that says 'Wannsee.'"

Shayndl was so tired, she was barely able to follow his instructions. In a weary voice, she asked him if he could write down the name. The official gave the threesome a sympathetic look and went inside the booth. In a moment he was back with a piece of paper in his hand and was followed by a young boy.

"Go to the station Bahnhof Börse. Here it is. He will put you on the right train," he said, pointing at the boy.

"Thank you," said Shayndl. "You are a true helper in need."

As she was picking up the suitcase, he barked at the boy, "Take that suitcase. You can't let a tired woman carry a heavy suitcase all by herself!"

"I'm sorry," the boy mumbled with a guilty look.

This is a good sign for the beginning, Shayndl thought as she carried Malka up the flight of stairs. It was only five minutes from Bahnhof Börse to Rosenstrasse. They left the suitcase with the caretaker at the entrance and followed his instructions to go upstairs to a certain office. Shayndl explained her situation to a man who promised he would search for Avram. Meanwhile, he suggested, she and the children could find shelter at the transit home on Heidereutergasse, just around the corner. She gave him a grateful nod.

For three days, she did not dare go out for fear of missing Avram. On the third day, she was called by the caretaker, who told her a policeman was there to see her.

"We found your husband, young lady," he said. "It took so long because he wasn't in Berlin at all. He had hired onto a ship in Hamburg bound for America." He hesitated, waiting for the effect his message would have. "But don't worry," he continued, "we caught him just in time and he's now on a train. He'll be here soon."

Shayndl could not believe her ears. When the policeman was gone, she sat down on a chair. Her heart was pounding. He was simply going to abandon her and the children! He left with the intention of leaving them behind in Kraków, penniless and alone! The day she had picked him up from prison, she had been ready to forgive everything, even trust him again as before. From the distant past, she heard her mother's voice: "He'll make you unhappy, my child. . . . As soon as you have children, he will leave you."

Had it been possible for her to go back to Lemberg, she would have done so then and there. But the road was blocked. Weary and dejected, she resigned herself to the situation. The police had played fate and were bringing him back. All right then, let it be that way.

A few hours later, Avram appeared in the doorway, flanked by two policemen. He seemed to be looking through his wife. Somewhat defiantly, he walked up to her. She avoided meeting his eyes and gave him a weak handshake. The girls, untroubled, rushed to meet him, glad to be able to cling to their father. And at this moment, he was glad to be able to cling to them.

The Jewish community gave them a starting allowance and they moved temporarily into a furnished room with use of the kitchen in Lichtenbergerstrasse between Friedrichshain Park and Strausberg Square. Avram found work with Mittler & Son, one of the "best printing houses in Berlin," so said their slogan. With his first paycheck, they rented a two-room apartment in Schmidstrasse near Jannowitz Bridge. It was a working-class neighborhood, but to Shayndl it felt "just like paradise," as she often said in later years. The toilet in the hallway was shared by only three apartments. It was kept clean and did not give off a ghastly stench like the one in the yard in Lemberg. People did not live closely crammed together as she had been used to. Shayndl stayed home with Malka and supplemented their income by sewing coats. Rebecca went to the neighborhood school and was placed two grades below her age. She needed time to learn German and to get used to the new country, the teachers said. Since she spoke not only Polish but also Yiddish, she learned very quickly. Soon she was talking like a true Berliner and could hardly be distinguished from the other children around her.

At times, Shayndl wondered about Avram, the one-time freedom fighter. She now asked herself: Had he been a swindler even back then? But she did not say this out loud. She had pushed the ax-wielding knight so far away that he no longer haunted her. She told herself: Just don't revive the old squabbles. In most things, he lived up to her expectations. She was grateful that he was good to the children and brought home the household money regularly. Sometimes, however, she woke from a deep sleep in the middle of the night with the feeling that her bed was a coffin. Only when she opened her eyes could she shake this feeling off. Even more difficult was to silence the voice that told her: You do not deserve to live!

Avram settled down. This big city was more exciting than any other he had ever known. He soon felt at home in Berlin. Many Eastern European Jews lived in the area between Friedrichstrasse and the Friedrichshain Park, most of them in what is today called the Scheunenviertel (Barn Quarter). Avram liked to stroll down Grenadierstrasse (today Almstadtstrasse) to browse in a Jewish bookstore, have tea and cake in a Jewish coffeehouse, and generally take in the scenery. He felt especially drawn to these streets because they reminded him of the Jewish quarter in Kiev. In every fourth house was a synagogue or a prayer room, for religious expressions from orthodox to liberal. The streets teemed with bearded men in long caftans, children at play, and beckoning prostitutes, who, however, were never Jewish. At least that is what every Jew would protest indignantly should anyone suggest the contrary. In the many corner pubs, the Berlin underworld was likewise at home. There was much buying, selling, hawking, and dealing, and there were also the many people who left early in the morning and came home late at night after a hard day's hard work in an office or a factory.

The closer Avram came to Alexanderplatz, the more elegant the houses became. Here there were fewer ground-level apartments and shops. Avram let himself be drawn into the hustle and bustle as he approached the city square with its large office buildings and department stores, the streams of people passing each other, merging together, and then separating again, the screeching and clatter of streetcars and automobiles, the chatter of voices.

The sun was shining, the air was warm; he breathed freer than he had in a long time. He did not feel like going home yet, where the girls would fall over him. He wanted to be by himself for a while, he needed time to think. When he suddenly found himself in front of the Alexanderplatz train station, he decided to climb the stairs to the platform. He had been told that if he wanted to get to know Berlin, he should ride the S-Bahn. He got on the next train and sat down on one of the lacquered wooden seats, curved to fit the contour of the human back. He stared at the automatic door. The

Avram in 1922.

opening and closing of the doors—with a sudden jerk, as if operated by an invisible hand—still seemed like a miracle to him.

The train began to move, and he made himself comfortable and watched the buildings fly by the speeding train. Behind Friedrichstrasse, the windows of the apartment buildings were so close to the railway line that he felt like an embarrassed intruder as he tried to catch a glimpse inside the apartments. But everywhere, even in the poorest tenements, his view was barred by white curtains—for him a sign of affluence. He sighed. If only he could get some money from somewhere. Then Shayndl would not grate on his nerves so much with her scolding and that hurt, grim look she now had most of the time. In the old days, when she still looked up at him, they had gotten along well. She had seen him as a knight in shining armor, a fairy prince. Now that she knows the real me, she is probably disappointed, he thought. It was useless to talk with her about this. All she felt was shame when he tried to do something for the family, as with the counterfeiting. He was right not to have told her anything about it. She may well have been dumb enough to cry her heart out on somebody's shoulder, and then everything would have gone bust sooner than it did. But then again, she did manage to support herself and the children for three years without me, he thought with admiration. That had given him the idea of going to America without her. What she was able to do for three years, she could certainly do a while longer. As soon as he had the means, he would have sent her money. Why make a stopover in Berlin if one can get to America directly? Alone, he would have gotten the money together much sooner. He was sure of that. But the German police had crossed his plans. Well, what can you do, he thought with a sigh.

At Bellevue Station the scene outside changed, and he was torn from his thoughts. The jungle of buildings had cleared. His view scanned the wide open spaces between the mansions and the splendidly adorned buildings near the Tiergarten. Here the gray buildings looked like little dots in a sea of green lawns and trees, interspersed with brilliant red, yellow, and blue flower beds. The passengers getting on and off at the Zoo Station were more elegant. Ladies with fur collars, shopping bags, and lapdogs in their arms hurried past his window in search of the dog compartment. Again rows of houses came into view as the train continued on. The streets were lined with trees. Everything looked so much better than on Schmidstrasse. Here were the residences of factory owners, businessmen, and high-level managers, artists, and independent professionals. Avram sighed. "Charlottenburg," he read, and, glancing at the S-Bahn map overhead, he saw that he would soon come to Westkreuz, where he would have to transfer to the Ringbahn.

When he was comfortably seated on the new train, the scenery changed again. "Schöneberg," "Papestrasse," "Tempelhof," "Neukölln," he read, as the train stopped at these stations. This was an industrial area with many small workshops in backyards and whole factories, big and small, surrounded by tenements. It was only behind Sonnenallee, toward Treptower Park, that there were fewer houses. Here lived craftsmen and better-off workers, lower-level civil servants, and office workers in stiff collars and black suits. One of them got on the train and sat opposite Avram, who suddenly felt himself being scrutinized with a severe, condescending look. He was glad that he had to switch trains again at Ostkreuz. Now he came to Warschauerstrasse and Schlesische Bahnhof. This is where he had first arrived in Berlin, he remembered. He got off at Jannowitz Bridge, where a ten-minute walk would take him home.

He suddenly quickened his step, overcome by a longing to see his children. He also felt that he should do something nice for Shayndl. He stopped at a neighborhood store and bought a sinfully expensive box of chocolates for Shayndl and candy for the children. As he was paying, the picture of three pairs of gratefully shining eyes appeared before him, and he was happy to have a family.

It was in 1930 that Shayndl received one of those rare letters from Uri. She made herself comfortable at the living room table. When Uri wrote it was always a long letter, filling her in on the latest about the various members of the family. Now, as she pulled a single sheet of paper from the envelope, she furrowed her brow, hoping it was not bad news. She read. Father had died! She felt the shock like a physical blow that knocked the breath out of her. "Papa!!" she gasped. The knight, bathed in light, appeared before her eyes again. Now the ax was gone. He simply looked at her severely. How she had longed for a reconciliation, had longed to tell him that he had been right about Avram! And now it was too late. Malka, who was playing on the floor, brought her back to the present.

"What is it, Mama?"

"It's all right," Shayndl said soothingly, as if Malka were the one who needed comforting instead of herself. "Uncle Uri wrote. He sends greetings from Grandma." Malka nodded. She had never seen either of them and wasn't sure what an uncle or a grandma was. Shayndl brooded a while longer. Then she pulled herself up heavily. At least I will be able to speak with Mama again, she thought with a sigh.

In 1931 Avram applied for German citizenship. For the moment he had put off his dream of America. It was impossible to save enough money to pay for passage for four people. And if he stayed in Germany, then he at least wanted to live without constantly having to worry whether the residence permit would be renewed. He waited impatiently for the reply. And when it came, it said no! Avram was angry. He had been living in this city for three years. He even had work, despite the world economic crisis, but they would not accept him as a citizen. He said bitterly, "There is just no room in this world for the likes of us!"

Malka suddenly pulled his sleeve. "For who, Papa?"

Avram, startled out of his thoughts, turned and slapped the child's face.

"Avram, what are you doing?" Shayndl screamed. Avram gave off a Russian curse and stormed out of the room.

A nostalgic yearning overcame Shayndl when she thought back. How tender her often ill-tempered husband had been when Rebec-

The Zwerling family in 1930.

ca was born. And how much joy Malka had given him before he had been arrested. Another child may save our marriage, she thought. Eight times she had been with child and—thinking of her mother—eight times she had seen to it that she would definitely lose it. This time, she decided, she would not interrupt the pregnancy. The decision became the anchor to which she would cling. It made the thought of a future with Avram bearable. All she wanted, after all, was to be happy again.

"I'm pregnant."

He gave her a puzzled look. "You don't mean to say you want to have this child?"

She nodded. "I don't have the strength for another abortion," she said with a weary look. "And besides," she added, looking for a reason that would make it agreeable to him, "it might be a boy this time. He will carry on the family name."

"But Shayndl," Avram tried not to seem too annoyed, "with a third child we would need a bigger place, and how would we pay for it?"

"Rebecca is going on sixteen; she will move out soon. I want another child." She knew she was lying.

"You can see what's going on around us. The Nazis almost rule the streets. That madman Hitler tells people that they are the master race and that the Jew is responsible for all their misery. You never know when the first pogrom will take place. And you want to bring another child into such a terrible world?"

"Avram, the Germans are not primitive, ignorant peasants like the Ukrainians. It won't be all that bad. Besides," she repeated, "I just don't have the strength to go through another abortion." She thought, once he holds the baby in his arms, he'll be happy. To ward off any further argument, she added reproachfully, "And anyway, why don't you take more care? You act as if getting pregnant is my business alone." She knew he had no answer to this.

He sighed and left the apartment without a word.

❀

Loni—Blond and Blue-Eyed

The child in her womb gave her little trouble at first. But in the hot summer days of the last month, Shayndl longed to be rid of the burden. One night, toward the end of August 1932, her time had come at last. She went to the Jewish hospital on Iranische Strasse in Berlin-Wedding. The labor pains did not plague her long. But the baby did not to want to leave the warmth of the womb. Rather than making its way into the world headfirst and being propelled through the tunnel by Shayndl's pushing alone, the doctor had to pull it into life by its feet. When she heard the first cry, Shayndl looked at the clock on the white tiled wall of the delivery room; it was almost ten in the morning. Exhausted and relieved, she looked at the bluish-red, wrinkled creature. The hair was blond and the eyes were blue. She didn't take after her own family. Must be Avram's, thought Shayndl.

"What will you name the girl?" the nurse asked.

Shayndl had thought about that for months. Here was an opportunity for a sign of reconciliation with her father, may he rest in peace. The child shall be named after him.

"Salomea," she said. The nurse looked at her questioningly. "After my father. His name was Shulim. If we were still in Lemberg, I would call her Shulamis—that is the feminine form of Shulim. But we are here, so I'll call her Salomea. That's German enough."

"But Mrs. Genin!" The nurse had a troubled look. "Don't you see what is going on here? Imagine your girl goes to school with such a Jewish name! That could be hell for her."

Could the nurse be right? She did not want to put obstacles in the child's way from birth. "What should I call her?" Shayndl asked helplessly.

The nurse thought for a moment. "Why don't you call her Loni?"

Yes, Shayndl thought, that's not too common and sounds like a normal German name that would not identify the child immediately as Jewish.

The birth register read "Salomea" but the child was always called

"Loni." Shayndl pronounced it with a heavy Slavic "L."

In later years, I hid my real, obviously Jewish-sounding name. I wanted to be called Loni. At the age of forty, in the course of my search for my long-lost identity, I insisted on being called Salomea. With the return to my name, I began to accept: I am Jewish whether I like it or not.

The day she returned home from the hospital, Shayndl already regretted having borne this child. She was exhausted. In the womb, the baby had been a physical burden; now it grated on her nerves. Breast-feeding tired her even more, so she discontinued it within a few weeks. She bathed, diapered, and put the baby to bed. She did her duty as a mother. But this child gave her no joy. Why is she so restless? thought Shayndl whenever the baby cried. She can't be hungry, she has also just been bathed; then she felt the baby's hands and feet, and they were warm. Wearily, she picked her up. The child looked at her expectantly and then started crying again. Had Salomea been able to speak, she would have said: "Mama, hold me tight. I'm freezing. Please keep me warm, Mama."

But Shayndl did not understand the cry for help, just as her own crying had not been understood in her infancy. So little and already wants to be pampered, she thought. That the child should need her smile, her caressing, her attention and warmth, did not enter her mind. How should she give the child warmth when she herself was frozen inside? Helpless, she put the baby down again and let her scream. Often, she wished the child would disappear. But she didn't. So they were both condemned to life.

Sometimes Avram played with Salomea. His face was beaming. Every touch, every glance was full of warmth and love. For him the baby was no burden. He did not have to look after her day after day. That was woman's work. When he had enough of the child, he got up and left.

Shayndl longed to stay in bed and sleep day and night. But somebody had to care for the child. Rebecca could not help. She was close to finishing her apprenticeship and spent most of her time at a workers' sports club. She was almost grown up and had no time. Her parents accepted this. Eight-year-old Malka was "only" a child. Her time, outside of school, belonged to them. Shayndl insisted that Malka take the baby out in the carriage after school so that she could get some rest. It was Malka who heard the first cries turning into screams when Salomea was hungry or wet. It never occurred to Shayndl that Malka might need some time for herself. Neither did it occur to Malka. Yet she often took her time coming home from school so that she could play undisturbed along the way.

As cute as the baby was—sometimes Malka would sit completely still and stare in fascination at the little fingers and tiny nails, at the pale blue eyes, so completely different from her mother's and her own, at the round face—Malka often felt burdened by this responsibility. But it never would have occurred to her to protest. Older siblings, especially girls, always looked after younger ones. That was natural. It had always been that way and would always remain that way . . .

And yet, she sometimes hated her little sister. When the baby was lying on her back, crying her heart out for no visible reason, Malka would yell at her to stop. If that didn't help, she would take her to Shayndl, who would pick her up to see what was the matter, and a glimmer of hope would flare in Salomea's eyes. Now I will finally be hugged, warmed, and comforted. But after a brief moment, she would again hear her mother's vexed tone: "Oh, there's nothing wrong with her. She just wants to be pampered. Go take her for a walk, Malka!"

So Malka went on her way with the disappointed child, who screamed all the louder. What a pain in the neck she was. If only she could just leave the baby at home or park the carriage somewhere in a corner and go away. But then her parents would get angry with her. She couldn't bear that. So Malka had no choice but to let the child scream and then complain about "that stupid Loni."

In July 1933 came the next catastrophe. Avram lost his job. "This best printing house in Berlin," he said sarcastically and deeply hurt, "probably wants to be *judenrein.* For years they were satisfied with my work and now, suddenly, they don't want me anymore."

Finding another job as a printer was hopeless. Avram answered a newspaper ad for salesmen by a lingerie manufacturer, one of the many Jewish textile companies located around the Spittelmarkt. He became part of a whole army of salesmen who, to support their families, went from door to door every day, offering their wares to the housewives.

I'll go where the money is, Avram thought, and, with suitcase in hand, he took the S-Bahn to Wannsee. He got off at Nikolassee and looked up and down the street. It did not matter whether he turned right or left. Everywhere were two- and three-story mansions surrounded by neatly kept lawns. The filthy rich, he thought with envy. He looked at the nameplates and tried to muster his courage. The bell was usually at the gate and the entrance to the house about twenty or thirty meters away. Some had signs next to the doorbell saying: "No soliciting." He rang anyway. A maid dressed in a black and white apron opened the door. From afar she saw his threadbare suit, his lined face, and the suitcase in his hand. She asked, "Do you want to sell something?"

He produced a friendly smile. "I have here very nice lingerie, best quality, lowest prices. You can afford it, too, Miss." If only he could speak German without an accent! He saw the scornful look on the girl's face.

"Can't you see that it says no soliciting?" the girl called out brusquely, and slammed the door shut.

Avram took a deep breath. He had not even made it past the gate. He walked on, dejected. How could he make it in this job? The plate at the door of one house read "F. I. Rosenthal, Counselor at Law."

Well, well, he thought, if the *I* doesn't stand for Isaac I'll eat my hat. He took heart and pressed down the handle of the gate. It opened! He quickly rang the bell and walked up to the door of the house. Again a maid opened. He decided not to tell her what he wanted.

"I would like to speak to Mrs. Rosenthal," he said firmly. The girl was very young and seemed new in her job. She gave him an uncertain look and closed the door, which was opened again almost immediately, this time by a slender, well-groomed, black-haired beauty. He suddenly had a picture before his eyes of Shayndl and the way she looked when they first met. If only the counterfeiting business had worked out. Then she, too, would be living today like this woman and would look like her . . .

Avram tried hard to hide his Yiddish accent. Servile, almost fawning, he said, "I am from the firm of Pinzker & Co." He put the case on his knee, supported it against the wall, and opened the lid. "We make very beautiful lingerie. Maybe you would like to take a closer look. I am sure you will like it."

The woman looked at him in disgust. "I suppose you're from the East, aren't you?" she said. Avram was startled; he felt caught red-handed and could only nod. From inside the house came a man's voice.

"Who is it, Esther?"

"Somebody selling underwear," she shouted. "He rolls his *r*'s like they do on bad radio shows."

"Oh, a Jewish salesman. Probably one of those poor devils from the Scheunenviertel. Give him something and send him off. And tell the girl to show Dr. Falckenberg into my study as soon as he arrives."

They're talking about me as if I weren't here, Avram thought, as if I were a beggar.

"One moment," the woman said. When she came back, she handed him a one-mark piece. "We don't need any lingerie, thank you. But here, take this."

Avram looked at the silver coin on his palm; it felt as though it were burning. Oh, that he could sink into the ground or simply become invisible! He quickly closed his suitcase and hurried back to the gate. Only when he reached the street did he slow down.

Now he was too discouraged to try again. But one mark was too little for a day's take. Three more times he rang a bell, but he sold nothing that day. At four in the afternoon, he took the train back to settle the day's account with the company. Downcast, he told of his experience.

"Where did you go? Nikolassee?" exclaimed the cashier, also an Eastern European Jew. "The German Jews want nothing to do with the likes of us. We're too dirty, ignorant, and primitive for them. They live over there in their big mansions, and we are here around the Alexanderplatz, so we don't bother them. You have to go to places like Brenzlauer Berg, Wedding, or Kreuzberg, where the poor live. The workers' wives have only two sets of underwear, usually of the cheapest sort, which wear out quickly. The wealthy buy ten sets at a time, and of the best quality. They would never buy from a door-to-door salesman."

For three more months, Avram tried to earn a living this way. Then the company sacked him. When he came home with the news, Shayndl just gave him a scornful look. He knew he was a failure and could not expect any sympathy from her.

Despite their plight, they did not have to go hungry. Avram collected unemployment, which was just enough to keep them alive. An application for rent tax reduction was granted, cutting the rent almost by half. Sometimes, when there was neither money nor food in the house, Shayndl would take the children to the Jewish community soup kitchen. In the company of other Jews, she was warm and friendly, listening patiently to their stories, and generally lending a helping hand wherever she could. Even though these encounters were temporary and brief, they helped her forget her loneliness for a while. Avram rarely came along. He hangs around and wastes his time, she remarked bitterly. She usually said this as she and the girls put on their coats to leave the house. Along the way she often fell into a brooding silence. The more Shayndl tried to fend off her depressed moods, the more she succumbed to them. She did not know that depressions come from bottled-up pain. Besides, she felt she was somehow to blame for all this suffering and felt guilty. Decades later, she said that she had been mentally ill then. She felt rejected and abandoned, and held Avram responsible. She felt chained to this man who kept her locked in a prison cell. The two-headed monster in her cowered, waiting for the ax to come crashing down. At home Shayndl hardly spoke a word, and her silence lay heavy over the whole apartment. Although she was able to pull herself together enough to run the household, she was rarely able to respond to her children's emotional needs. Everyone got on her nerves, and she wanted to be alone. The two youngest had no choice but to live with her depressions, and they also felt rejected and abandoned.

One day Avram made clear how much Malka was responsible for the welfare of her sister. It was toward the end of the summer of 1933, and the family still lived on Schmidstrasse. Malka took the baby to the nearby park of the Märkische Museum. To make it safely across the busy Neanderstrasse, she had to ask passersby to help her. She was so small for her age that she had to stand on her toes to look inside the carriage. Salomea, by contrast, was heavy and fat for her twelve months, and still could not walk. If Shayndl had been forced to expose Malka to malnutrition, Salomea was to have it better now, she determined, and she was proud of the baby fat. Salomea sat like a lump in her carriage, watching Malka play with other children. Suddenly she felt a sharp pain in her finger. A boy was biting down on it. She gave off a shrill scream. Malka came running up and chased the boy away. Then she hurried home, for the bite mark was blood red and might need bandaging.

At home, she first ran into Avram and explained what had happened. His face darkened. Suddenly his hand came down on her with a hard slap. He shouted, "How could you let this happen?" Malka's little body flew from the door where they were standing across the room to the window on the other side. Frightened and in pain, she cowered whimpering against the wall. Shayndl ran into the room, alarmed by the noise. When she saw what had happened, she gathered Malka into her arms and glowered hatefully at the man who had once given her so much love. It was all a lie! Avram's eyes wandered from the two to Salomea, who was sitting, frightened, on the floor. His anger melted when he saw her. He turned around and left the room as if it were he himself who had been struck. Salomea watched him leave, her wide eyes full of fear. Her father had turned from a god of all-embracing love into an unpredictable, fear-evoking demon. And Malka, her protector, had proved to be weak and vulnerable herself.

This nine-year-old child, who was herself in need of warmth and affection, had to find the strength—but where should it come from?—to be a mother to her sister. When they were alone again, Malka planted herself in front of the cowering child with her legs apart and her hands on her hips. Her anger exploded. "I have you to thank for this," she screamed at her. "Papa hates me, Mama is always in a bad mood, and I have to drag you around like a *hoiker*, a hump on my back, all the time." Suddenly, Salomea felt two slaps on her face. The next moment, Malka, shocked by what she had done, rocked the frightened child in her arms.

Five decades later, my sister assured me that she had not "minded at all" being responsible for me. She denied ever having hit me, although my later memory tells me she did so more than once. "I loved you more than any-

thing," she told me. What such incidents instilled in me then, however, was the lasting sense of being unbearable because she could not bear the burden of responsibility for me.

✿

A Small Jewish Shop, Opened in 1934

One day Avram came home and put five hundred Reichsmarks on the table. His eyes beamed at Shayndl triumphantly. "We'll open a shop. From now on we'll be able to live like human beings," he said.

Shayndl turned pale. The shock of his arrest in Kraków gripped her again, and she asked apprehensively, "Where did you get this?"

"Don't ask so many questions. Just be glad it's here."

She thought for a moment. Actually, she would rather not know where the money came from. She said, "You want to open a shop? Jewish businesses have been boycotted for the past year! What makes you think you can make a go of it?"

Avram waved her words aside. "That's only against big department stores like Tietz and shops in better areas like Charlottenburg. We'll move to the poor section in Wedding. They'll leave us alone there. I've thought it all over," he concluded firmly.

Shayndl realized that once again he had made a decision without consulting her and nothing she could do would stop him. But where did the money come from? For a long time this question continued to weigh on her mind. Much later she heard that Avram and a friend had broken into a safe, and the two had divided the loot. She was deeply ashamed and at the same time glad that it was not discovered.

They moved to Gottschedstrasse in Berlin-Wedding, into the rear rooms of a sundry store. There was much that delighted little Salomea. She enjoyed sitting on the counter and fishing yellow cake tasting of aniseed from a glass bell jar. She was allowed to eat as much as she liked. And her father was always there with her. Every time Shayndl threw Salomea's pacifier into the burning stove with the remark, "You're three now and too big for this," he always gave her a fresh one from the box. The whole family knew that Salomea was Daddy's favorite. With him around, she could do anything. He never lost his patience with her.

Business was good. They had enough to live. And Shayndl, now wife of a Berlin Jewish businessman, felt an inner peace she had never known before. She had the feeling of standing outside of herself and watching what was going on around her as if it were a motion-picture show. Again and again, scenes from the past came back to her: her fight to marry this man, the wedding, his arrest, the three years alone while he was in jail, also the good moments of those years, then his departure from Kraków, the journey to Berlin, the shock of his betrayal, and his angry outbursts, his unjust behavior, especially toward the children. Again and again the thought came to her mind: I have been married now almost twenty years. I have chained myself to this man for all this time. I'll be forty soon. What have I gotten out of life and this marriage? Three children and a lot of unhappiness! Half of my life or even more is already over. What am I to do with the rest? She had no answer to this question. But she was not to have much time to ponder it. Not in this Berlin, not in such a time.

One morning—it was the spring of 1935—Rebecca had left the shop to go to work when she was in for a big shock. She had to maneuver around an SA man in brown uniform to reach the street. Around his neck he carried a poster that reached from his shoulders to his hips: "Don't buy from the Jew!"

Avram, too, was shocked when he saw the man. Are they already penetrating into the (politically) "red" Wedding? Not a single customer came all morning. Only when the SA man left in the afternoon did a few customers dare enter the shop. Then the SA set up a regular post in front of the shop. Fewer and fewer customers came. The unsold goods had to be dusted more often.

Malka, too, experienced difficulties at school. She knew nothing about the law passed on April 25, 1933, that limited the number of Jews at universities to 1.5 percent. However, she did read a poster that remained glued for a long time to the many advertisement pillars all over Berlin. "Against the un-German spirit" read the headline. "A Jew can only think like a Jew. When he writes German, he lies . . . Lies must be stamped out . . . the Jew must be outlawed as an alien . . ." She giggled when she read: "Jewish writings must appear in Hebrew. Whenever they appear in German, they are to be marked as translations. Drastic action must be taken against the misuse of German writing." She saw herself as the only one in her class writing in Hebrew. What nonsense, she thought.

As it was considered too much to expect others to share a classroom with children of this alien, parasitic race, no more than 10 percent of the children in public schools were allowed to be Jewish. Not many Jews lived in Wedding, so Malka was not expelled and did not have to go to one of the few overcrowded Jewish schools, as happened to so many children who lived in the Scheunenviertel. Instead, she was banished to the left corner of the classroom and had to sit on the "Jew's bench," as the teacher, Herr Scholz, called it.

Herr Scholz was not a popular teacher. He was insecure, given to angry outbursts, and he disciplined the children in the firm belief that only if they were afraid of him would they become decent human beings. They had to obey, and those who did not were lashed with a cane. He also hoped to curry favor with the school principal with his "Jew's bench," for only the approval of his superiors gave him a sense of importance.

From time to time he would give a lesson in race studies. First he explained how evil the Jews were, how they exploited and fooled the German people by dominating and controlling both the press and publishing industry.

"Now, the Jew has launched a hate campaign against us abroad and is spreading all kinds of horror stories about us. He slanders us as 'Huns' and 'Barbarians.' The Jew press claims that in Germany communists have their eyes gouged out, that people in protective custody are being tortured to death, and that we hold pogroms against the Jews. The Jew carries on his shameless boycott campaign against German products. We must defend ourselves against this. That is why there is a boycott of Jewish businesses and the Aryanization of their companies, for the only way one can get at the Jew is by hitting him where it hurts, in his bankbook."

Then he had Malka come up to the front of the class. "You can recognize the Jew immediately by his physical attributes," he lectured. "For example, by the measurements of his skull." With his pointer he highlighted the various body parts as he discussed them. "A sure sign is the attached earlobe." Malka instinctively raised her hand to see if he was right. A sharp pain, caused by a slap with a cane, made her withdraw it quickly as her classmates laughed. Herr Scholz promised to bring in a scientific skull-measuring instrument one can use to distinguish the higher from the lower races.

Malka stood in front of the class and looked into the many faces. For more than a year I have been together with them every day, she thought. They know me! They can't possibly believe all these things about *me!* Soon she was forced to realize how wrong she was. Not long after the "Jew's bench" was set up, the "Jew's corner" was added in the schoolyard. Since they were cut by the others, the few Jewish children from all grades gathered there.

In constant fear of malicious heckling or stone throwing, they stood around mostly in silence, or they spoke softly with each other. When the attackers came closer, the bigger children placed themselves in front of the smaller ones. They had already learned that bullies are usually cowards who pick fights only when they think there is no risk of harm to themselves. Malka, too, pushed herself to the fore. Although she was small and slight, she was already eleven years old and wanted to protect the younger ones.

One day, out in the schoolyard, a fourteen-year-old boy said to her, "You know, I only learned last year that I'm Jewish. No one ever talked about it at home before. And now my big brother is on a farm, preparing to go to Palestine. He's studying Hebrew and runs around with one of those little caps. He has become religious!" He let out a grim, ironic laugh. "Actually, it was only them," he jerked his head toward the center of the schoolyard, "who turned us into Jews."

"I've always known that we're Jews," said Malka.

"Yes, but you're from the East. There the difference between Jews and the others is obvious. Your parents speak Yiddish, don't they?"

Malka nodded and added, "Also Polish, and my father Russian."

"There you are. But we're Germans, like them." Again he jerked his head toward the children on the playground. "But now we're no longer allowed to be that." He paused and then added, "Well, soon it won't matter to me. We're leaving, probably also for Palestine. Then they can all lick my . . . "

Malka sighed. She did not understand her classmates. All right, they were afraid of Herr Scholz, but was that a reason to cut her during break? She wanted to know exactly where she stood.

When she came home from school that day, she did her home-

work, then took Salomea by the hand and took off. Four girls from
her class had always played with her after school. They, too, had to
take care of younger siblings, and they often got together at a nearby sandbox, where the little ones played while the older ones talked
within view. At least that's the way it was until the "Jew's bench"
was set up. From then on, the others avoided her. She decided to
look them up at home. With neither teachers nor other classmates
around, she would find out whether she was really as lonely as she
felt.

She rang the first doorbell. Brigitte opened the door. "Can you
come down to play?" asked Malka.

"I'm not allowed to play with you anymore," said the girl. Sneer-
ing and scornful, she added, "And don't ever come back here again."
The door fell shut.

Liesel, too, opened the door herself and looked at Malka with
her eyes wide open, as if she were seeing a ghost. "What do you
want?" she asked, glancing apprehensively down the hallway.

"I wanted to ask whether you would come down and play with
me," said Malka.

"No, my parents won't let me play with Jews. You'd better go or
I'll get into trouble." She, too, closed the door without waiting for
an answer.

Malka looked sadly down at Salomea. She did not have the
courage to call on the other two. "Come on, let's go home. They
don't want us."

A sense of coldness enveloped them like a cloud as they walked
along the street. When she got home, Malka saw that her father was
busy in the store, so she went immediately into the living room in
the back. Downcast and close to tears, she stood in the door, still
holding her little sister's hand.

"What's the matter?" Shayndl asked with concern.

"Biggi and Liesel won't play with me anymore, nor will anybody
else in school. Liesel says her parents won't let her play with Jews."
Her voice almost choked. Tears rolled down her cheeks as she
looked at her mother in helpless despair.

"Mama, I'm sitting on a Jew's bench." Until then she had not
said a word about the gauntlet she had to run in school every day.
Her parents were always so preoccupied with their own problems.

Now it all came out at once: the race theory lessons, the hostility during break, how she hated going to school.

Shayndl was looking at misery. It did not occur to her to take her daughter into her arms and comfort her. "Don't pay any attention to it, Malka. You'll just have to pick your friends from among the Jewish children." She thought of her own childhood and knew she never had such problems. She played with her siblings, and where she grew up there were plenty of Jewish children. Besides, it would never have entered her mind to want to make friends with a shikse. She just presumed that a non-Jewish girl would not want to have anything to do with a Jewish girl.

At the dinner table, Shayndl told Avram Malka's story. He listened grimly. If the children are like this, then this country is becoming unbearable, he thought.

"The Jewish girls' school is in Auguststrasse," said Shayndl. "She would have to take the train, of course, but don't you think we should send her there?" She turned to Malka. "What do you think? I hear it's a good school." Her eyes moved from Malka to Avram and again back to Malka. Avram nodded. Malka sighed, thought for a while, and then also nodded.

After the half-year report in October 1935, Malka started at the new school. Even though she was now able to breathe freely inside the building, it was all the worse outside in the street. Hostile children often waited in front of the red-brick school for their Jewish "enemies." Their abusive taunts and humiliating insults pierced Malka's soul like pointed daggers and left lifelong wounds.

When even the Christmas season of 1935 did not bring in enough to cover the debts, Avram realized he would have to give up the shop. The fact that it was not his fault alone did not make him feel any better. Although Rebecca was almost never home—she had met a young man named Horst Faber at the sports club and spent most of her time with him—and she earned her own keep, it hardly lightened the burden. Avram's irritation and uncontrolled outbursts increased. He never discussed his problems with Shayndl. He knew she would only become hysterical and shout at him. In March 1936, it became clear that he would not be able to pay the rent. They would have to move. He would have to tell Shayndl soon and that frightened him.

While reading the advertisements in the newspaper one morning, he got an idea. A "well-to-do widow, good-looking and affectionate," was looking for a "husband with a good business sense." Bigamists were not unusual. Maybe this is a way out, he thought. He even toyed with the idea of divorcing Shayndl so that he could support her and the children secretly with the widow's money. And if he got some pleasure out of it, all the better. In a letter he described his good sense for business and suggested a meeting.

Every day he lay in wait for the mailman so that the answer would not fall into Shayndl's hands. It came five days later with the first mail delivery at eight in the morning. The widow suggested a rendezvous for the following week. He nodded happily. He would keep that appointment. As he crossed the hall between the shop and the room in the rear, he stuffed the letter into the pocket of his jacket—or so he thought. In his excitement he did not notice that it was only the envelope and that the letter had fallen to the floor. Thank God, Shayndl was still in bed, he thought.

But she was already awake and sitting at the edge of the bed when he entered the room. On the way to the bathroom, she automatically picked up the piece of white paper on the floor, glanced at it, and could not believe her eyes. She read the letter three times. It was not her usual despair that gripped her, but a cold fury that broke out from inside. This was the last straw! The betrayal eight years ago when he almost left her for America, and now this! During the last few months, standing beside herself and seeing herself acting out her life, she had toyed with the idea of separation. At this moment, the idea turned into firm determination.

She returned to her bed and pondered the new situation. Salomea, too, had now woken up and slipped, as she did every morning, into her parents' bed. She saw that her mother was brooding again, so she stayed on Papa's side, happy that she had the big featherbed, which still breathed some of his body warmth, all to herself.

Avram came back into the room. When she saw him, Shayndl was unable to contain her anger.

"So I'm not good enough for you anymore?" she exploded. She waved the letter and screamed at him: "You moral cripple!" Salomea started with fright. She saw her mother jump out of bed and, in her nightgown, hurl herself against her father, who was standing at the door. She wildly pummeled his chest with her fists, and the two started to wrestle with each other. He had street shoes on! If he steps on Mama's toes, he will hurt her terribly, Salomea thought, horrified. Mesmerized, she stared at the quick movements of the two pairs of dancing feet, one pair barefoot, the other in shoes. For a few seconds, they filled the whole room, and there was nothing else in the whole world but these feet. Suddenly the struggle abated. The room returned and the feet again took on their normal size.

A terrified Salomea now looked into the faces of her parents. Her Papa left the room, her Mama went back to bed and stared motionless at the ceiling. Shayndl's fury had subsided. All she felt was a cold emptiness. The two-headed monster sat exhausted in its corner. You don't deserve happiness, it grumbled. Her father's cold eyes, as they were saying good-bye, looked down on her from the ceiling. Silently she asked his forgiveness.

Shayndl looked at Salomea. It's a good thing that children don't understand, she thought. So she did not see her child's fear, and it did not enter her mind to hold or comfort her. And because the little girl was left alone with her fear, it turned into an empty loneliness that remained stored in the underbelly of her soul, protected by forgetting.

Fifty years later, in the middle of a psychotherapy session, I remembered the incident. My therapist gave me the strength to find the courage to allow the forgotten fear to reach me. I cried the uncried tears. Now the adult Salomea could comfort Loni, and some of the loneliness disappeared.

As early as the age of three, Salomea learned that she must not show weakness. So mother and daughter pulled themselves together, got dressed, had breakfast, and began a seemingly normal day. But for Shayndl everything had changed—she no longer felt herself to be Avram's wife.

In March 1936, Rebecca brought home her friend Horst and declared: "I'm moving out, Mama. I'm going to live with him. This is no life around here." She inclined her head in the direction of the store where Avram was. Shayndl nodded. She is right and old enough. But . . .

"But Rebecca, this is illegal! The two of you could be arrested for this."

"Nobody at Horst's place knows that I'm Jewish."

"My child, I hope it all goes well."

As Rebecca was packing her things, Shayndl realized that Horst had not come along merely to help carry the suitcase.

"Mrs. Genin! You should leave Germany." His voice sounded urgent. "Rebecca and I often think about it. We want to get married, but the Nuremberg laws won't let us. This is no passing spook, as some say. The boycott and Aryanization are only the beginning."

Shayndl looked into the bright, intelligent eyes. A likable goy, she thought. They cannot get married. Well, Rebecca would be better off marrying a Jew anyway. Rebecca set her packed suitcase down by the door and joined them at the table. She agreed with Horst. "Yes, Mama. I think we should leave Germany."

"But where would we go?" Shayndl asked. "What country is willing to take in stateless Jews?"

"Couldn't one of your brothers help?" asked Rebecca.

Shayndl thought out loud, "Uri is in Brazil, Bezalel in Australia, and Mottel is in Palestine. I'd rather not go there." Uri as well as Bezalel had made a stopover in Palestine, and through their reports she knew how difficult life was there. Only Mottel had settled there. It seemed bearable only if one had no family and shared his Zionist fervor. She knew she would be alone with two children. Palestine was out of the question.

"Brazil wouldn't be bad, if they let us in. Uri wouldn't be able to help us. He has two children of his own, and he makes a living selling used books from a pushcart. His customers are mostly students at the university. The best thing would be to write to Bezalel. He has a grocery store and could support us at first. But even if the Australians let us in, how would we get there? It'll cost a fortune."

"Mama, we'll ask the community for help. They help people emigrate. Maybe they'll help us, too."

Shayndl nodded. Yes, these *yeckes,* the German Jews, they may not want to have anything to do with us, but ever since we've been in Berlin, the community has never left us in the lurch whenever we have been in real need, she thought.

When the young couple was gone, she lingered, steeped in thought. Her plans for the future became clearer. She wanted a divorce. But wasn't she obligated to stay with Avram for the sake of the children? Even against her will? She longed for a good long talk with her parents. Her father was dead, but her mother was still liv-

ing in Lemberg, and most of her siblings were there, too. Yes, she
decided, she would go to Lemberg to ask her mother's advice and
get the addresses of her brothers abroad. She would have to take
Loni. She couldn't leave the little one in Malka's care. Fortunately,
she was not yet four and didn't need a train ticket.

The next morning, she simply told Avram that she wanted to go
to Lemberg for a reunion with her family. Avram was surprised, but
he only nodded. Her tone and attitude showed a determination and
strength that reminded him of the time when he came home from
prison. He took a good look at her. Her face showed wrinkles that
had not been there before. In fact, she looked almost haggard. Very
few traces remained of her former beauty. She said, "Believe it or
not, I'm looking forward to seeing Lemberg."

❖

"Not Another Hour with You"

Being cooped up in the compartment of a train for twelve hours would have been torture for Salomea had they not traveled at night. On this journey, the child experienced a rare feeling of being safe and secure. Her mother did not seem so stressed as she usually was. In fact, she was almost cheerful. Even when Salomea got tired and wanted to sit on her lap, she was not pushed her away. As she was falling asleep, Salomea felt her mother's breasts like soft pillows under her head, the soothing warmth of her body, and the protective firmness of her arms. She was being held at last.

While Salomea fell into a deep, peaceful sleep, Shayndl remembered her last journey eight years ago in the opposite direction and how she had carried the other daughter, then also four years old, in her arms. How much lighter Malka had been, almost skin and bones. How hard she had had to fight then for every scrap of food for her children. She enjoyed the plumpness of this daughter, whose body weighed against her thighs and pushed against her stomach. Yes, Berlin is a good place to live, she thought, as the monotonous rhythm of the turning wheels sent her off into a light doze, although ready to wake immediately in case her daughter started to slip from her lap.

At Grandmother's apartment, Salomea was bombarded by a host of new impressions. So many people in such a small space. With eyes wide open in astonishment, she took in this strange world. All the family still living in Lemberg had gathered to welcome Shayndl. Mottel, too, happened to be visiting from Palestine. So much joy, so much shaking of hands, so much embracing! Again and again Salomea was lifted up, kissed, her cheeks pinched, until it hurt.

"Loni, this is your Uncle Duvid, Uncle Lemel, Aunt Golda, Uncle Yisroel, Uncle Mottel. And here is your Oma."

Salomea looked at the shriveled old woman with the graying hair and stooped shoulders. She looked stern. The woman seemed to try to smile at her, but in vain. Salomea pushed against her mother. Who was this woman? What is an Oma? "Go on, give her a kiss, Loni." No, she couldn't do that. She hid behind Shayndl and clung to her skirt.

"Let her be, Shayndl," she heard the woman say. "She will get used to things around here and then she'll come to me."

Relieved, Salomea came out of her hiding place, but she stayed close to her Mama.

All these people in the small apartment were mostly preoccupied with their own business, so Salomea could do what she wanted and was rarely scolded. No one paid much attention to her, except her Mama. And her Mama was so different from the way she was back home in Berlin. She responded to Salomea's questions, took her along wherever she went, even to the Yiddish theater, where she actually managed to stay awake until they got back home shortly before midnight.

Sometimes there was joking and laughing, something unknown to Salomea from home. When she saw her Uncle Duvid eat for the first time, she watched in amazement. She had never seen anything like it. With each bite, his mouth and eyes opened and closed simultaneously. He left a deep impression on her with his long, grizzled, wild beard and his wavy hair. As they sat around the table, she looked at him a good long while and then suddenly said, "He looks like a king." They all burst out laughing and from then on Duvid had his nickname.

When she could not get what she wanted, she would break out in loud, piercing screams, and that was very disturbing in the small apartment.

"Can't you bawl a little louder?" Mottel asked her once when she was screaming.

Surprised, she stopped and said matter-of-factly, "I can holler like a lion."

"How loud? Show us!" Now she was allowed, no, expected, to scream as loudly as she could. She took a deep breath and let go. They all put their hands over their ears and laughed. It turned into a game, the likes of which her Mama had never played with her. Now she had to laugh herself, and she forgot what it was that had started her crying in the first place.

The only thing that bothered Salomea was the one toilet in the yard that served all the occupants of the building. The stench took her breath away, and the little hut made her feel sick. She got into the habit of holding on as long as she could. Often she did not make it in time. Even though it was unpleasant to have to show her mother the wet pants, Salomea was relieved when Shayndl did not scold her. She just nodded with understanding, washed her, and put on fresh panties. Wetting her pants became a habit, and it took a whole year before Salomea was "dry" again.

One day she went with Uncle Mottel to the edge of town. A two-meter-wide serpentine path led up a hill. From the top she looked down and could see the whole city. Holding her mother's and uncle's hands, Salomea hopped and skipped first up and then down the path. All this time, Uncle Mottel spoke urgently to her mother.

"Come to Palestine, Shayndl. We need as many Jews as possible to build a Jewish state there. You can come without Avram and live on a kibbutz. There will be work for you and everything you need. And the children will be taken care of as well. I'm going back in three weeks."

"No, Mottel. The best thing for me is to join Bezalel. I asked Mama what she thinks. She agrees that I should get a divorce and then find the money for the passage to Melbourne."

Mottel gave up. He knew he could not compete with advice given by the mother with whom Shayndl was reconciled at last.

Back in Berlin, Shayndl immediately went to the Jewish community. She spoke of her situation as if she had already left Avram. Yes, they could find work for her, she was assured. Many Jewish households were looking for cleaning women since the Nuremberg laws prohibited Jews from employing non-Jewish servants under forty-five. The community was also willing to give her a small monthly child-support allowance. Salomea could be placed in one of three Jewish nursery schools. And as for emigration to Australia, she should apply in writing for a sum to cover the passage. Shayndl nodded gratefully. She had not yet written to Bezalel. Her first concern had been financial independence. Leaving Berlin was second.

Shayndl found a furnished room for herself and the girls in Dresdner Strasse. As she started packing, Avram came into the room and watched her.

"What are you doing?" he said surprised.

"I'm moving out."

"Where to?" He could not believe it.

"You'll find out when I've filed for divorce!" She gave him a cold, contemptuous look.

Avram sank down on the nearest chair. His anger rose. "You have another man who can give you more money than I can, you slut!"

The silence in the room threatened to explode. Seconds seemed like years. Shayndl took the suitcase in her right hand and with her left she reached for Salomea. Avram felt pinned to his chair by her contempt. Never before had she shown such strength. Her words echoed in his mind long after she and Salomea were gone: "I'd rather be dead than spend another hour with you under the same roof!"

Shayndl sat on the bed in their rented room, with Salomea on her lap and Malka standing next to her. She was physically and mentally exhausted. Good, it was done! She looked at her suitcase and then she looked around. The furnishings were shabby, and the room was dark and depressing. Once before she had been in such a room, had experienced such a relief, and at the same time such profound unhappiness. That was at the start of her marriage. This here was the end. Tears welled up in her eyes, and Shayndl held tight to Salomea. But this time she did not break down as she had in Budapest, for she was ashamed to cry in front of her children. Salomea had never seen either Papa or Mama cry. The child felt her mother clinging to her and would have liked to slide off Shayndl's lap and flee from the room. But where to? Salomea wanted a cheerful Mama, the way she had been in Lemberg.

"I want to go to Papa," she said, hoping that this might be a way out. Shayndl did not answer. "Aren't we going back to Papa?" Salomea insisted.

Shayndl searched for words to help the child understand. "Papa is a very selfish man. I don't want to live with him anymore. But you don't understand this . . . " Again Shayndl fell into brooding. Soon she turned to Malka. "Please take her for a walk." Malka did as she was told.

In the house on Dresdner Strasse lived a girl named Helga, who was a year older than Malka. She, too, had to take care of a younger brother. Helga's mother always welcomed Malka when she came to their door with Salomea after school. The woman was moved by the sadness in the girl's eyes. She had a "big heart and a big mouth," as one says of Berliners. She cared nothing for racial theories or ideologies. Was somebody hungry? Was somebody unhappy? She had a nose for misery, and what her own family didn't use in food or strength, she gladly gave to those in need. From then on, Helga became Malka's only non-Jewish friend.

They lived in this dingy room for three weeks. Whenever Shayndl was not out looking for an apartment or cleaning somewhere, she sat around, staring into space. She did not notice how often she overlooked the needs of her child, just as Shulim and Dvoire had not seen *her* needs. She was unaware that her own unhappiness was being passed along an invisible umbilical cord to which Salomea was still attached. For her Salomea was just a plain nuisance. When she needed something and did not get it, she cried; then she was even more of a nuisance.

"You're just as selfish as your father," she would hear her mother say in a bitter, reproachful tone. Not only was this enough to make the girl fall silent, it also told her that her selfishness, her evil nature, was something she had inherited at birth. It was a curse she would never be able to escape. In order to avoid coming into conflict with her mother, Salomea also had to turn her father into a devil. She came to accept the notion that she was to blame if nobody loved her. In the following weeks, the little girl, not yet four years old, gathered all her strength to hide the evil half of herself—for was she not attached by a two-pronged umbilical cord to both parents?—in a dark, sealed chamber like a prison cell.

In later years, I did not know that a part of me lived in this closed cell. Only when I fell in love and the hope arose with it that I could escape my loneliness did the door open. Then I panicked, for through the open door my true self would become visible. My lover would now be able to see the two-headed monster I felt myself to be, and I was sure he would turn away. I did not know that from the earliest months of my life I had learned: You don't deserve to be loved and that is why you are being abandoned. And because I did not know it, the fears of the small child took control of my actions. I hid my fear behind a mask of indomitable strength. I felt my own pain as my lover's cruelty, and I raged to defend myself against his "abuses." Thus, I drove him away or I left him. I was relieved when the cell door fell

shut and I could withdraw again into loneliness. Every reenactment of that
childhood trauma confirmed my conviction that I was to blame if nobody
loved me. I was more than fifty years old before I came to realize, in the
course of psychotherapy, that, for me, love and fear were two sides of the
same coin.

Shayndl found an apartment on Lietzmannstrasse at the corner
of Georgenkirchstrasse not far from Alexanderplatz, on the out-
skirts of the Scheunenviertel. It was a bright apartment on the third
floor, with three rooms, one of which Shayndl decided to rent out.
The kitchen was large, and the corner bedroom had three windows
with a view onto the streets below.

They soon became accustomed to their new life. Shayndl took
the train every day to Charlottenburg, where she worked for four
hours cleaning the apartment and office of a Dr. Simon. Malka
attended the Jewish girls' school in Auguststrasse and, on her way,
she dropped Salomea off at the nursery school.

When she added it all up, Shayndl was amazed how much
money she actually had: her wages, the rent from the room, and,
added to all that, the allotment from the Jewish community. Four
weeks after the separation, she thought over her situation and knew
she had done the right thing. The children did not have to go hungry a single day. She was proud of herself. She was very happy to be
rid of Avram. Life was much better without him.

One day Shayndl came home from work and found a letter from
Avram. She read it in the kitchen and then ran into the living room
to Malka. The now-twelve-year-old girl was not only a substitute
mother for Salomea; she was also Shayndl's substitute partner, and
she was proud to fill both roles.

"Malka, just imagine what your father has come up with now!"
Shayndl declared with a mixture of amusement and indignation.
"He insists that I give him the allotment from the community. And
do you know why? So that he can make his business profitable for
the two of you. He still seems to think that we're coming back." She
shook her head. "He's really meshugge!"

She ignored the letter and filed for divorce. The next thing she
heard that had to do with Avram came from the police. She was
notified that her husband was in prison, and since she was his only

relative, she was requested to come in for an interview. His residence permit had expired and would not be renewed. Avram was a stateless, penniless Jew, and it was therefore impossible to deport him. Although he was willing to emigrate, he did not want to go without his family. The police wanted to know how she felt about it, since they were separated.

"No!" Shayndl answered firmly. "I have filed for divorce." Even though she, too, had plans to leave the country, she would go where she would be out of his reach! She visited him in prison to make the situation perfectly clear to him and to disabuse him of any hope of a future together.

A week later his residence permit was unexpectedly renewed, and he was released with the warning to get out of Germany as soon as possible.

When she heard from him a third time, it became clear to her that he had really gone meshugge. It was in mid-July 1936. This time the notice came from a mental institution in Wittenau. Again, since she was his only relative, Shayndl was asked to appear for an interview.

She sat quietly, her hands folded in her lap, in front of the massive desk of Dr. Britzer. "Well, Mrs. Genin, your husband has been committed to our institution on grounds of being a menace to the general public." Shayndl looked up, surprised. "He wrote a letter to the welfare department of the Jewish community." He paused. "You are receiving financial support from the community, right?" Shayndl nodded. "He demanded that the money be paid to him, as the head of the family, rather than to you. He threatened to 'blow out the brains' of the head of the office, and then his own, if the community did not come to his aid."

"I can't imagine that he would be capable of doing something like that," was Shayndl's comment.

"We think so, too, but we must be certain. We can't completely dismiss the possibility that he'll be a danger to himself or others. He needs somebody to care for him."

"Doctor, I don't want to have anything to do with my husband!"

The doctor, in his white coat, leaned back in his chair and thought for a while. He looked at Shayndl as if he were trying to look inside of her. "You lived with him for twenty years," he stated

matter-of-factly. Shayndl nodded. "You also have three children."
"Yes."

"Your husband needs you now. Every time he is questioned about
his family, he bursts into tears."

"That's just like him," Shayndl burst out angrily. "Doctor, this
man is a very good actor!" She told the doctor how awful her life
with Avram had been. While she spoke, her eyes flashed with anger.
"This man is obsessed with money. We don't count for him. If he
says he needs us, he's lying."

The doctor took a deep breath. She is very bitter, he thought. But
I have to tell her about the disease. "You have children," he stated
again very matter-of-factly.

Shayndl nodded. He knows that already, so what! she thought
with growing impatience.

"Your husband contracted a luetic infection in 1916. It can be
passed on. You should have your children examined, just as a precau-
tion."

Shayndl gave him a puzzled look. "What's that, a 'luetic infection'?"

"Syphilis. You know what that is?" Shayndl's face turned flaming
red. She certainly knew what that was! 1916? The year they got married, the year Rebecca was born? In other words, when he was sleeping with her, he must have been going to prostitutes on the side.
And she heard about it only now! She cursed the day she had first
laid eyes on him. The doctor was still speaking. She forced herself to
concentrate. "Although the disease was treated, medical science did
not have the means then to cure it completely. I should imagine that
he has become more difficult in recent years, that his temper has
become more uncontrolled. Can you confirm this?"

Shayndl nodded.

"He is now in the third stage, which involves brain damage. We
shall try, nevertheless, to cure him with mercury. This has been very
successful in many cases, and it takes about a year. And then, it
would be best for him to be reunited with his family . . . "

"No! Absolutely not!" Shayndl screamed. She shook her head vio-
lently. "This is too much to ask, Doctor. I don't care where he goes,
and under no circumstances will I take him in."

The doctor shrugged his shoulders. There was nothing else he
could do. Shayndl left.

When she got home, she had to lie down. She closed her eyes and saw once again the ugly, two-headed monster cowering in fear and hatred before the knight. But the knight's face was covered with open wounds and scars. She heard the spiteful laughter as he swung the ax and carved a deep wound into the formless body. She rested for a while but could not calm herself. When she got up, the hatred rose in her again. For weeks she ranted and raved against this man, and again she begged her dead father's forgiveness. Over and over she called him a moral cripple, who had not only ruined her life but, on top of everything, had been so irresponsible toward his own children. How was it possible that he had kept this disease from her for so long? Salomea listened. She knew her mother's fury was directed at her father, and she pushed yet another piece of the inherited evil into the airless, lightless cell.

To Shayndl's relief, it turned out that none of them had been infected. Nevertheless, the children would have to be observed for some time, said the doctor, in case the disease was only latent.

Avram's letter had frightened the official at the Jewish community, who had informed the police. That is how Avram landed in Wittenau. After nine months, he was transferred to an affiliate institution in Ilten near Hanover. Avram saw in all this nothing but a personal, anti-Semitic attack against him. His patient record at Ilten stated: "Orderly in his thinking. Speaks with a foreign accent. Endeavored to become a German citizen, but failed . . . Constantly makes special demands—typical Jew. Not aberrant in a psychotic sense . . . "

This is how it came about that Avram, in despair, wrote to his doctor: "Dear Dr. Meyer. You once told me that you are nothing more here than a physician. This led me to believe that every attendant under your direction was nothing more than an attendant. But this is not the case. The attendant, Herr Gedecke I believe is his name, has persecuted me since he learned that I am a Jew. I believe that he has the sympathetic ear of his supervisor. I would not have cared much about the change in my sleeping quarters were it not for the fact that I know it happened as a result of slanderous remarks this gentleman made about me to his superior. In addition, there are many other smaller forms of harassment whenever this gentleman is on duty . . . "

Shayndl received a card asking her to come to the Central Berlin Court in a matter concerning her divorce. Would Avram get leave for this date? Maybe they would try to bring about a reconciliation? She showed the card to the doorkeeper. He looked at the room number. "Here, to the right and upstairs," he pointed to a curving staircase in the foyer, "then to the right to the first exit. From there one more flight up and to the left. You can't miss it," he explained.

Shayndl was filled with a sense of awe as she climbed the stairs to the second floor of the forbidding, confusing building. She turned down a corridor with many doors on both sides. Here and there, an officious-looking clerk, with files clamped under his arm, came out of a door, hurried past her, and disappeared again inside another. One could see from the expression on the clerks' faces that important business was being done here. People's future hung in the balance; their fate was being sealed here.

She walked and walked and walked, and again found herself at the stairs in the foyer. Again she had to ask for directions. She stopped the next official who came into view. He was going the same way, and he showed her to a stairwell that could be reached only by an inconspicuous door. Oh, she had overlooked it. Finally, she found the right room, and paused briefly at a window before entering. Outside, on the wall opposite, was written in large letters: "Mercy without favors, firmness without hatred!" Nice principles, she thought as she knocked on the door. If only they existed in real life! She was relieved to find the official alone, without her husband present.

"All we need to know from you, Mrs. Genin," he said, after he had offered her a seat, "is whether you still insist on the divorce." She nodded. "All right. Then we can be brief. We shall set a date and let you know."

For this I had to come all the way down here, Shayndl thought, annoyed. She shrugged her shoulders and left, going back the same way she had come. This time she made sure not to miss the door to the stairs.

Out in the street, she thought about this building. A real labyrinth. Long corridors leading nowhere or back to where you started; the high, vaulted ceilings and the thick columns, so wide that someone could lie in wait behind them. Now she knew what had made her so uneasy since she had entered it: this building was meant to intimidate. She was glad that she did not have to come here to stand trial.

When Shayndl returned in September 1937 for the actual divorce, the children waited for their mother downstairs in the foyer. Salomea held on to Malka's hand and looked around. She had never seen anything as beautiful and splendid. This is how she imagined a royal palace to be. There were two curved staircases that merged in front of a huge, stained-glass window that covered the entire rear wall from the ground to the second floor. There was an artistically molded railing and tiles on the floor, each imprinted with a royal crown. In the center of the foyer stood a bronze statue of a king on a horse.

After a while Salomea became restless and asked, "What are we waiting for, Malka?"

"Mama is getting a divorce," was the reply. Even though Salomea did not know what that meant, Malka's voice was so somber and sad that she did not want to ask any further. It seemed to her that she had been standing there for hours. She passed the time by trying to discover new details on the railing or the floor and by watching the people go by.

Shayndl received a letter from Avram: "Since my doctor told me yesterday that you wrote him a long letter in which you declared that you had no intention of taking me in, since we are now divorced, and since, as a result, they will not let me out on leave, you will have to come to Wittenau and set the record straight. If you want, you can bring this letter. The fact that we are divorced is no reason not to let me out on leave . . . I ask: Whose interest does it serve to keep me locked up here? Nobody's, except perhaps that of the asylum in Ilten. But this asylum has more than a thousand patients. I'm sure they won't go broke without me. My doctor seems to believe that it violates some higher principles if he doesn't put obstacles in the way of a Jew. He obviously forgets that this Jew has done more for the fatherland than many a German who loudly proclaims his patriotism."

As she was reading, Shayndl shook her head. What did *you* ever do for this country? she thought. The fact that you are now working here has to do with your treatment . . . But since there was no

one else who could help, Shayndl decided to take him back in. On
paper. For the authorities.

꧁

"Good that We're Getting Away from Here"

It was the end of September 1936. Shayndl had picked up
Salomea from nursery school. She was walking along Georgenkirchstrasse, holding the child by the hand. A few steps from
home, she saw a thin, pale woman sitting on a chair, a child about a
year old on her lap, and another, about Salomea's age, standing next
to her. Helpless and shivering from the cold, she sat there, staring
into space with dull, expressionless eyes. She has probably been
evicted because she couldn't pay the rent, Shayndl thought. She felt
sorry for her and remembered how she felt the first few months
after Avram had been arrested and before she found work. She, too,
could have been out in the street had it not been for that generous
landlady, or if the Jewish community did not help her now. Hesitantly, she walked up to the woman.

"Can I help you?" she asked.

"Would you have a room for us? Maybe a bowl of hot soup?"
The woman spoke without hope.

Shayndl remembered that the extra room was empty at the
moment. Why should the woman not live there until a new tenant
was found? Shayndl said, "Come with me, we'll arrange something." Shayndl led the way with Salomea, and the woman with her
children followed behind.

At home, Shayndl showed them into the kitchen and she put
water up for tea. From the door Salomea eyed the group as they sat
around the family table. They were strange to her. She didn't mind
their presence, but she didn't know what to do with them.

While Shayndl took cups and plates from the cupboard, put
bread and cheese on the table, she saw the stiffness leaving the
woman's body and tears flowing down her cheeks.

"Why are you doing this?" the woman asked, obviously puzzled.
Shayndl looked at her, taken aback. This woman is not Jewish, she
thought. She asks because she herself would never think of doing
something like this for others. A Jewish woman would immediately
have opened up to me, would have taken me into her confidence,

and would have made herself at home in my kitchen. Shayndl did not know what to say. To gain time she asked back, "What do you mean?"

"Well, that you took us in and you're giving us food to eat."

"Should I leave you out in the street?" It sounded like a reproach.

"Others passed by and not one paid attention to us. Why you?"

What should she say? She felt obliged to help Jews in need. All right, Frau Otto was not Jewish. She did not realize that she had learned this attitude in the tight-knit, protective community of the shtetl. Here was a woman who needed help, so she gave her a helping hand. If I were in her place, I would probably wait in vain for her help, Shayndl thought. She pushed her discomfort aside. So what, she thought, she can't help it. After all, she is German. Out loud she said, "I was once in such a situation myself. I know how you feel."

The woman continued to cry softly. "Go on crying. Sometimes it's good to cry." Shayndl placed a calming hand on her shoulder. "I happen to have an empty room right now."

The woman began to sob. "You must forgive me. I'm not used to so much kindness." Then she told her story. Her husband had been beating her, especially when he was drunk. Then he left her without a penny. Everything of any value she had pawned long ago, but it hardly brought enough for food, let alone rent.

"What is your name?" asked Shayndl.

"Otto, Inge Otto, and these are Hans and Gertrud." She pointed at the two children.

"My name is Genin, Zelina Genin." She used the Polish form of her first name, because it was less conspicuously Jewish. "For the time being you can stay here, Frau Otto, until you have found some other place."

Frau Otto again shook her head, bewildered. "How can I ever repay you?" Suddenly, she gave Shayndl a penetrating look. "You're Jewish, aren't you?"

Shayndl started. Had she taken an anti-Semite into her house? She nodded unwillingly. Then she saw with relief the grateful smile on the face of the other woman.

"I thought so, because of the way you speak. I'll never forget what you're doing for me," Frau Otto said.

Shayndl showed her the room with the big double bed and helped her change the linen of the featherbed.

During the two weeks Frau Otto and her children stayed with them, Salomea observed the family from a distance. Gertrud clung anxiously to her mother's skirts, and the little boy, too, sought no contact. Salomea noticed that it was not long before the two women ran out of things to talk about. They both strained to be friendly, and the effort was clearly noticeable.

One Saturday, Shayndl awoke with stomach pains. A good thing it was Shabbat so she did not have to go to work. During the course of the day, she developed a fever, and by afternoon she took to her bed, excusing herself with: "I'm sure it'll pass quickly if I get some rest." She lay there, sick, weak, and remote. Salomea played with her doll. Frau Otto fixed supper that day and then called everybody to the table. Salomea was glad to be sitting next to Malka. She would have felt very uneasy alone with Frau Otto and her children.

When Salomea's bedtime came, she heard Frau Otto ask Shayndl, "Frau Genin, would you like Loni to spend the night with us so you can get some rest? After all, sleep is the best medicine."

Shayndl thought briefly. The woman was right. Without the child she would have more peace of mind.

Salomea watched her mattress and bedding being moved into the other room and put on the floor. She let herself be undressed by Malka, but the thought of having to leave her mother and sister made her afraid. Malka bent down and wished her a good night. Then she disappeared. Salomea knew they were right next door, in the adjoining room, but what kind of a room was this? She did not know it, and everything was so strange and cold.

When the lights went out, she buried herself deep inside the covers. She listened to Hans and Gertrud, who were in the room with her, whispering. The strangeness, the coldness, closed in on her. She began to cry for help. "Mamaaa! I want my Mama!" Instead Frau Otto came in.

"You needn't cry, Loni. Mama is right next door. She is sick, so leave her be. You don't have to be afraid." Her voice was severe, and Salomea could hear how hard she tried to sound friendly. Salomea dug herself deeper into the pillows.

"I want my Mama," she cried again.

"Oh, don't be ridiculous. You know she is right next door," Frau

Otto said impatiently and left the room.

Salomea continued to cry softly. Abandoned! Those she needed did not want her.

After a while Frau Otto came back. "But Loni, I told you there is no need to cry."

"I want to go to my Mama," Salomea sobbed.

"You're disturbing Hans and Gertrud with your crying. They have to sleep, too." She crouched next to the mattress and smoothed the featherbed with her hand. "Sleep tight now." And that was exactly what Salomea could not do. For a long time she continued to cry softly into her pillow.

Around ten o'clock, Malka finally came in. "All right," she said gently, "if you can't sleep without Mama, then you'll just have to come back over." Salomea got up and trotted barefoot into the next room. There she found her bed pushed right next to her mother's. Deeply relieved, she lay down. She only had to stretch out her hand to touch Shayndl. Happy, she looked into her mother's feverish face. The strangeness was gone, calm had returned. With a deep sigh, she closed her eyes and immediately fell asleep.

Two years later, Shayndl and Salomea saw Frau Otto again. They were walking along Georgenkirchstrasse when Salomea suddenly saw Frau Otto coming toward them, holding Gertrud's hand. Salomea looked at her mother. The smile of recognition on Shayndl's lips suddenly froze. That's funny, what's the matter with her? thought Salomea. She looked back to Frau Otto, who suddenly changed direction and was just stepping off the sidewalk to cross the road. Hastily pulling her daughter behind her, she kept her eyes trained straight in front of her.

"Mama, isn't that Frau Otto?"

"Yes, Loni." The answer came with a deep sigh. "Don't take it to heart," she said with a pained smile. It sounded as though she were trying to console herself. "She's not a bad person. She's probably afraid to say hello to us." More to herself than to Salomea, she added, "Good that we're getting away from here."

The new tenant was a forty-year-old man named Czernik. He was an unstable person whose good luck had brought him to Shayndl, as he said. He quickly sized up the situation: a woman separated from her husband, still burdened by two children, and blinded by a desperate need for love. All he had to do was give her a little hope, a bit of sweet talk, and she would melt into his arms. As long as he managed to hide his illness—his alcoholism—from her, there would be no problem.

He had a rival in thirteen-year-old Malka, and she was not blind. Since the separation, she had become Shayndl's confidante with whom she discussed all family matters. This was a good substitute for the affection and comfort Malka had always missed. Since Shayndl slept with the two girls in the corner room, it did not escape Malka that her mother often came to bed very late. It also did not escape her that Herr Czernik and her mother flirted in the kitchen. She even called him by his first name, Heinz. When Malka woke up one morning and found herself alone in the big double bed, she knew he had gotten her. She was furious. How dare this man take her mother away from her!

In the morning she saw Shayndl leaving Czernik's room in her nightgown. How could she not be disgusted by this *yeckishe* drunkard! Doesn't she see that he drinks? Had Czernik not been a Jew, Malka would not have cared. But then Shayndl would never have taken an interest in him, and it would not have mattered if he were a drunkard or not. All her life, Malka had heard that Jews don't drink. This man got drunk regularly, staggered home, and never knew the next morning what he had been saying or doing the night before. It was simply disgusting! He betrayed everything Jewish and thus also her, who every day defended herself and the other children in front of the school against the "Aryan superrace." How could her mother get involved with such a man? She would give her a piece of her mind at breakfast.

"Mama, do you know that Czernik is a drunkard?" Her face glowed with jealous anger. Shayndl blushed. This conversation was not pleasant for her.

"That's an exaggeration. He likes to have a drink now and then, but that doesn't make him a drunkard."

Malka contradicted her sharply. "Anybody who comes home loaded as often as he does is a drunkard." After a pause, she added contemptuously, "How can you go to bed with such a man?" Shayndl's face now turned dark red.

"You're too young to understand this, Malka. When you're older, you'll see it differently."

"I don't think so!" Malka said with unconcealed disdain. She got up, took her schoolbag, and left, slamming the door shut behind her.

A year after Czernik had moved in, Shayndl woke Malka at five o'clock one morning. The unheated room was cold and dark. Shivering, and yet oblivious to the cold, she stood at the bed and shook Malka by the shoulders.

"Malka, wake up! Get dressed and go immediately to Rebecca before she goes to work!" Hearing the panic in her mother's voice, Malka was immediately wide awake. She knew that something serious must have happened, and she reached for her clothes.

"What happened?"

Crestfallen, barely able to contain her tears, every word a self-reproach, Shayndl quickly told her. "Before he came home drunk last night"—now she, too, pronounced the word "drunk" with contempt—"Czernik went to the police station, and he told them that Rebecca is living with Horst. She must get away from there immediately."

Malka was horrified and triumphant at the same time. She knew it could mean prison for both of them. But she had been proven right about Czernik!

She rushed out into the cold, her head clear, fully aware of the importance of her mission. She rang Horst's doorbell loudly. Rebecca lit the gas stove in the kitchen to heat the room a bit, and the three gathered at the table. The gist of the matter was quickly told. Rebecca and Horst looked at each other, frightened.

"You're still registered at your mother's address," Horst said. Rebecca nodded hastily. "So if anybody asks, then you have never lived any place else." He thought for a while and added, "The man has never seen me, and your mother will hardly have given him my address." He turned to Malka. "Does he know my name?" Malka shrugged. "If not, that could be our saving grace. They can't get to me at all, and you can deny everything and tell them that these are the wild fantasies of a drunkard."

Hope flared in Rebecca's eyes. Hastily, she packed her things. A last, brief parting embrace. Then the two sisters were out in the wintry streets, lugging the heavy suitcase past the houses where the first-shift laborers were just leaving for work. Rebecca looked around, hoping that nobody who could denounce her to the police would see them.

An hour later, Shayndl, Malka, and Rebecca were gathered at the kitchen table in Lietzmannstrasse. It was not quite seven o'clock. Czernik was still asleep. While Malka was away, Shayndl had started to make breakfast, but now she could not swallow a single bite. She choked with fear and remorse.

"What does he know about Horst?" Rebecca had just asked.

"What does he know about Horst?" Shayndl repeated and tried desperately to remember what she had told him. "I don't remember exactly. I think at most I mentioned his first name. I'll ask him when he wakes up." She looked at Malka and added sadly, "Of course, I'll give him notice. I don't want anything to do with him anymore." Malka nodded, satisfied.

At this moment, a sleepy Salomea trotted barefoot into the kitchen. This reminded Malka that she had to go to school soon. The half-child got up, picked up her little sister, felt her feet, which had become cold, and said with a half-scolding and half-concerned tone, "How often do we have to tell you to put on slippers when you get out of bed?" She carried the heavy child back into the bedroom, put the slippers on her, and got herself ready for school.

When Czernik woke up, Shayndl questioned him. To her relief, he did not even know Horst's last name. Turning to Rebecca, she said, "You're officially registered here, and from now on we'll pretend that it has always been so. If they come around to ask questions, we'll deny everything. But now, Rebecca, we'll have to see to it that you get to Australia as soon as possible."

She had received a letter from Bezalel, promising to sponsor them all. Shayndl's thoughts concentrated on the numerous formalities that would have to be taken care of. The community was willing to pay for the passage. She was about to list all that was still to be done—provided the police heard nothing about Horst—when she saw the face of her oldest daughter and the silent despair in her eyes. She read her thoughts: What? Leave so quickly? Without Horst? Would she ever see him again?

To distract her, Shayndl said, "We need to apply for your passport, the Australian entrance visa, the exit visa, and a transit visa for Italy. We'll have to book passage on a ship, the fare has to be picked up at the community center, and you need a train ticket to Genoa."

Rebecca nodded mechanically. She knew all this anyway, and what she forgot, her mother would repeat. She preferred to wait and see whether the police actually came before making any move. She rose when she heard her mother say, "Now you have to get to work. Otherwise they may get suspicious."

A few days later, a policeman appeared at the door. His superior had sent him. "If we send her an official summons, she'll quake with fear and dish out some kind of a lie. If we catch her unawares, we have a better chance of getting at the truth," he had been told.

"Good evening, Frau Genin." He tried to give his voice a calm, factual tone. Shayndl nodded. "I am here in a matter that concerns your daughter Rebecca. Is she at home?" Again Shayndl nodded. "Could I speak with her?" Shayndl showed him into the living room, offered him a chair, and introduced Rebecca to him.

"We have been notified that you are living with an Aryan," he said. "You are, of course, aware that this is a criminal offense."

Rebecca was pale but calm. Shayndl was gripped with fear. Too much was at stake here for her to leave her daughter alone. Indignant, she interrupted him.

"My daughter would never live with a man without being married! And certainly not with a German. We know it's against the law! Where on earth did you get such nonsense in the first place?"

"That I can't tell you. But, actually, I wanted to hear *your* answer, Fräulein Genin."

"You can see that I am living here with my mother. Whoever told you this is a liar."

"Ah, I know who it was," Shayndl interjected again. "That drunkard Czernik. What nerve, spreading lies about my daughter! That was his revenge. You must know that I had to give him notice because he tried to paw her. When she put him in his place, he became vicious. So now he made up this story."

"Frau Genin," said the officer sternly, "your daughter is twenty-one years old and of age. She can speak for herself, can't she?"

"Excuse me," mumbled Shayndl.

Shayndl, Malka, Salomea, and Rebecca in 1938, just before
Rebecca left for Melbourne.

He turned to Rebecca. "Is this the way it is, Fräulein?" Rebecca
nodded silently with an embarrassed face. "You have nothing to
add?"

"No," she said firmly. He got up, and Shayndl showed him to
the door.

When she came back, they exchanged meaningful and relieved
glances. Shayndl took a deep breath. "Well, we got through this—
for the time being."

In January 1938 Rebecca left for Australia, where she stayed with
Uncle Bezalel in Melbourne. She never saw Horst again. Fifty years
later, she said, "When I left Berlin, I died my first death." The pain
of that forcible separation lasted a lifetime.

Autumn 1938. Since they lived so close to the largest and most
beautiful synagogue in Berlin, Shayndl decided to go there on Yom
Kippur, the day of atonement and forgiveness. Shayndl was not religious. She even doubted the existence of God. After all, had He
ever helped her in her need? Uri had taught her that God helps only
those who help themselves. Her father's religious fanaticism, as she
interpreted his sitting shiva for her, and the pain it caused her, had
led her to abandon all Jewish customs and rituals. However, she
now felt she owed it to her father—after all, he had been right
about Avram—her family, even to herself, to remember the traditions at least on this day.

She chose her clothes with great care, made sure Malka put on her best, and Salomea, too, was prettied up. Thus the threesome, Salomea holding onto Shayndl's hand and Malka walking alongside—my God, this girl is already as tall as I am, Shayndl thought—made the fifteen-minute walk to the synagogue.

The sidewalk in front of the synagogue in Oranienburger Strasse was overflowing with people: The women showed off their best coats and elegant hats, some had silver fox collars draping their shoulders; the men wore dark suits, and many wore top hats. The three went up to the women's gallery and sat down. While they were waiting for the service to begin, Shayndl was relaxed and content. But as the first sounds of the chanted prayers reached her ears, she was suddenly filled with an icy coldness. She wanted to flee from the hall, but she remained seated, as though paralyzed. Salomea almost slid off her lap. A horror of everything around her crawled up from inside. She remembered her father chanting and praying. Had it not been youthful rebellion that had caused the clash with her parents? Would she have insisted on marrying Avram if her father had not been so adamantly against it? Oh, Papa, if you only had met me with a little understanding, she thought, tears pressing against her eyes. How she longed for a reconciliation! She buried her mourning deeper in a corner of her soul, where it turned to stone. She sat there and held Salomea tightly pressed against her body. The cold seeped into the child and enveloped them both.

From the time I was thirteen, I refused to enter a synagogue. Almost fifty years later I met Judith, a rabbi's wife, who was a guest in East Berlin during the High Holidays. We took a liking to each other. "Why don't you come to the temple tomorrow?" Judith asked. "I'll be there all day. You don't have to fast if you don't want to. Just come for a few hours before the breaking of the fast and keep me company." I went. The seats next to Judith were occupied. I sat on the wooden bench behind her. The coldness again filled me. However, the warmth of this woman gave me strength. Suddenly the tears began to flow. For a long time I cried, heedless of the stares of those around me. As in the fairy tale of the Snow Queen, I felt an icicle melt in my soul. At long last I was able to mourn—for my mother's suffering and for the unhappy child I once was. It was two hours until the breaking of the fast. For the first time in decades I felt no aversion to being in a synagogue. The chanted prayers, familiar from childhood, filled the sanctuary and made me listen to the voice inside of me. Slowly I felt the cold vanishing, and I opened myself to an unfamiliar warmth that reached my soul for the first time.

November 9, 1938. It was getting dark early. Outside it was wet and cold, and Salomea enjoyed the warmth of the kitchen as the family gathered for supper. A sudden knock on the door made Shayndl jump from her chair. She latched the chain before she opened the door a crack. She recognized the Jewish neighbor who lived on the floor directly above. Pale and out of breath, he stammered, "They've herded three hundred Jews into the synagogue and set it on fire!"

Salomea imagined the flames bursting through the roof and lighting up the evening sky. The neighbor warned them not to go outside. In silence, they watched him leave. The conversation around the supper table was muted. Would they drag the families from their apartments? When they had finished eating, they went into the living room, which faced onto the street. The noise of marching columns, goose-stepping boots, the clatter of shop windows shattering reached their ears. Would the marching steps come to their door? Would the bell ring? They waited in tense silence—and were spared.

The next day Shayndl, Malka, and Salomea went for a walk. All of Berlin was out in the streets. Where the pavement had not yet been swept, they had to pick their way through glass shards strewn all over the sidewalks.

On Friday November 11, 1938, all of Berlin read this announcement in the *Morgenpost:*

> Last night the German people gave vent to their just and understandable indignation over the cowardly assassination of a German diplomat in Paris. In countless cities and towns, retaliatory strikes were carried out against Jewish buildings and businesses. We sternly call upon the entire population to immediately cease all further demonstrations and actions of any kind against the Jews. The entire Jewry will receive a final response to the Jewish assassination in Paris in judicial proceedings and official decrees.
>
> Joseph Goebbels

Now Goebbels took his time. Many had seen the burning syna-
gogues, had heard the cries of the injured, the deported, and the
slain. The next morning they had felt the crunch of broken glass
under their feet. Would the Germans protect the German Jews and
the Eastern European Jews among them as the people in Holland,
Bulgaria, and Denmark were to do a few years later? No. They did
nothing. The large majority accepted Goebbels's declaration un-
questioningly. Many felt satisfied that someone finally stood up to
"the Jew." Others, who did not need a scapegoat, just pushed what
they had heard and seen far from their minds. The few who protest-
ed disappeared, and few Germans cared to know where they had
gone. The panic-stricken neighbor's story about three hundred Jews
having been burned in the synagogue proved to be a false rumor,
but a prophetic vision.

Shayndl received a letter from Uri in Brazil:

> Since I read about the pogrom in Berlin, I am very worried about you.
> Were you affected? From what I hear, "only" men were taken to the
> camps. Please hurry up, leave the country! You know, Shayndl, I also
> fear for Mother and the others and their families in Lemberg. There is
> also talk of war. But they make no plans to leave. We, the younger gen-
> eration, left Lemberg a long time ago. But older people are probably
> waiting, like Papa did, for the Moshiach . . .

❀

I Remember

Mama, my sister, and I are walking along Georgenkirchstrasse, watching the people and looking into shop windows. We go into a bakery. I get a "sow's ear," my favorite. I catch the falling crumbs of puff pastry and stuff them into my mouth. It is one of the rare moments when I feel at ease with the world. I am five years old . . . My childhood vanished, or seemed to do so. For decades the pictures of my childhood were locked inside my head as black-and-white snapshots, frozen stills of an old movie that had suddenly stopped reeling. When I began to write down these memories and concentrate on these stills, many of them came to life and filled with feelings, with an overwhelming fear I had not known for fifty years. Only then did I realize that forgotten fear had driven me in making many of the most important decisions in my life. Wherever I found the courage to once again enter the hell that my childhood so often was, wherever I was able to shed the unwept tears and begin to feel for the lonely, wounded child I once had been, that is where the tight knot of self-rejection began to unravel. Then the pictures of my childhood took on color, moved again, and breathed life. Where I was unable to do this, the pictures in my head remained black and white, frozen and confined.

Summer 1936. "Come, Loni," Malka said one afternoon. "Put your coat on. We'll meet Mama at the station." Obediently, Salomea trotted along on her short little legs, holding Malka's hand. They walked to the Alexanderplatz and waited at the exit to the S-Bahn. Shayndl's face lit up when she saw her children. "That's a nice surprise," she said. Together they made their way back.

It was not easy to cross the Alex. Masses of people streamed in opposite directions, and if you did not watch out, somebody was likely to bump into you; then there were the cars and the streetcars crisscrossing the square. It took presence of mind to maneuver through all this. Salomea did not walk between her mother and sister as usual, but held her mother's hand while Malka followed behind.

All went well until they had passed the streetcar island in the middle of the roadway. They were just covering the next stretch to the other side of the square when Salomea was suddenly hit in the eye by a hard object. She screamed out in pain. Shayndl and Salomea looked around. All they saw was the rear of a heavy, bulging burlap sack on the back of a slightly deformed man in shabby clothes. He wedged his way through the crowd without looking to the right or left and disappeared from sight. He was probably carrying firewood for the winter, and a corner of his load hit Salomea in the eye. Shayndl poured out a flood of Yiddish curses on the unsuspecting man. "Anti-Semite! Criminal! *Mir veln im hobn in dr'erd,* into the earth shall he sink!" Salomea, holding her hand over the painful eye, thought: Oh, so that's why he hurt me, because I'm Jewish. During the next few days, the eye turned first red, then blue, and finally green. Shayndl applied compresses to ease the pain.

October 1936. Salomea was happy in nursery school. For the first time in her life she had playmates her own age and new toys to play with. She was already more than four and a big girl now. Soon she knew the way so well that she was trusted to go to school alone. She was proud but also glad that she was no longer being pulled along by Malka with impatient reprimands to walk faster. She took her time. Had anybody told her when she should get to her goal? There was so much to see along the way. She left the house, turned left, crossed Lietzmannstrasse, passed the corner with the laundry in the basement—Mama had sometimes taken her along, and she was allowed to hand her some of the lighter things, while Shayndl ironed the bed linen with the big steam press. Then she walked along Georgenkirchstrasse, continuing on the right-hand side. Just before Barnimstrasse was the hairdresser, who often joked with her when she came in for her regular haircut about the soft down that grew down to her neck.

"A real lion's mane," he said, and tickled her with it before he trimmed it.

"I can yell like a lion, too," she said proudly.

"But not here, please, or the house will collapse," he replied.

She was always happy when he looked out through the big shop window as she passed by in the morning. Then they would wave to each other. A block further on, between Barnimstrasse and Hoechste Strasse, was a toy store. All she had at home was one doll, one that had lost its head long ago. She did not mind, for she loved the doll just as much even without a head. She had made up a little ditty for it. Sometimes she stood in front of the corner window in the bedroom, looked down at the bustle in the street, and sang with her doll in her arms:

> my doll without a head,
> my doll without a head,
> my doll without a head
> listens to me . . .

Sometimes she stood for a very long time on the iron grid in the sidewalk in front of the toy store. How does one play with such wonderful things? Will the grid give way underneath me someday? Will I fall into the cellar and break my bones? she wondered. But it never happened. When she had seen enough, she moved on and finally came to the nursery school, some days an hour late. Aunt Meta greeted her with "Oh, come on in, Loni. I thought you were staying home today." With a smile, the teacher then made her join her play group.

Winter 1937. The children walked hand in hand across the Friedenstrasse to play in the big park, the Friedrichshain. The playground was fenced in by about twenty centimeter-high iron bars, which Salomea could step over with ease. One day in 1938, the fencing disappeared. Well, she thought, as she stepped from the lawn onto the footpath without having to lift her feet, iron is needed for war. She did not know what war was, but she had heard the adults talk about it. In her mind, she pictured a huge yard with piles and piles of iron bars.

Sometimes Aunt Meta called the children together for a group game, and sometimes the children were allowed to romp as they pleased. Just romping around was difficult for Salomea. She had never learned how. And this caused problems, especially in the winter. She just stood there, shivering from the cold. When Aunt Meta told her, "Loni, you'll be cold if you just stand around in the snow. Go play with the others," she took a few steps, but she did not know what to do with herself. She felt awkward and helpless; the others were quick and wild. She just couldn't keep up with them. Not knowing what to do, she soon went back to the teacher and stood motionless; her toes were hurting from the biting frost. When she started crying, friendly little Aunt Meta shook her head, not knowing what to think.

"Why don't you run around in a circle to warm up?" she asked.

Salomea did not know what to do and kept on crying. She breathed a sigh of relief when the children were called together and they returned to the warmth of the nursery school.

Winter 1937. After lunch was nap time. A row of cots was set up for the children to sleep on. But Salomea was not always able to sleep. Sometimes, to while away the time, she played with the big lips between her legs. That was fun. One day, she was stroking herself this way when Aunt Inge, the younger, slender teacher, suddenly appeared before her. She leaned over her and said in a growling whisper, "What are you doing there?" Salomea was startled, but she felt no guilt. She quickly pulled her hand from her panties and looked up at Aunt Inge without saying a word. "Don't do that again!" said Aunt Inge. Then, giving her a friendly look, she covered Salomea up and said gently, "Touching there is dirty. That's where the peepee comes out." Salomea heard her words, but thought: So what! She turned on her side and waited patiently until it was time to get up.

Sometimes Salomea imagined she was in hell and bands of little devils were pinching her with their fingers or with various delightful instruments. The others saw a good little Salomea sitting at the table or playing on the floor—but in reality she was experiencing a great and exciting adventure . . .

On the toilet she was always alone and knew she would not be disturbed. Sometimes she played with herself despite Aunt Inge's warning. Once she had made the discovery, it was much too enjoyable caressing herself between the big lips to stop. One time, she felt a great urge to stick toilet paper up her anus and wiggle it around inside.

Suddenly Shayndl came bursting through the door. "What are you doing there?" she asked sternly. Salomea was laid on the bed and the paper was pulled out. She heard a worried Mama say to Malka, "What will become of her if she starts as early as this?"

Winter 1937. Friday night was bathtime for millions of families in Germany, including the Genins. Shayndl set a tub, big enough for Salomea to fit in comfortably, in the middle of the kitchen floor, and heated water in a big kettle and in several pots. The first to get in was Shayndl. She was just able to sit in the tub and needed little water because of her size. When she was done, more water was added, and it was Malka's turn. Only then was Salomea allowed to get in. She didn't like it at all that she had to bathe in water that was swimming with the dirt that had washed off her Mama and sister. How she longed for clean water. "That's too expensive," said Shayndl.

One evening she was sitting in the tub, waiting for her mother to wash her, when she suddenly heard a scream followed by quick scurrying. She turned around and saw Shayndl standing on a chair, staring at a tiny little mouse, which was staring fearfully back at her. Then it streaked through the room and disappeared inside a hole under the wooden molding along the floor. Why is she so afraid of a mouse? Salomea wondered.

Spring 1937. Salomea had been in bed for five days. She had caught the flu and had been running a fever. At long last she was free of the fever.

"Mama, can I go out into the street? I haven't been downstairs for so long," she begged.

Shayndl felt the child's forehead. "Well, all right. But only with your coat and scarf."

Salomea went down the three flights of stairs and stood in front of the door. To the left she saw the basement laundry at the corner and to the right she looked toward the sandbox in direction of the Alex. She watched the comings and goings on the street. Oh dear, what was that? She listened to her insides. Had she gotten up too soon after all? She felt a wave of heat rising to her head. The fever seemed to be coming back. Her lips were hot and dry. She tried to wet them with the tip of her tongue. Suddenly she felt a hard slap on her face. A girl of about ten, whom she knew by sight, stood directly in front of her. Where did *she* come from? She yelled at Salomea, "You dirty Jew! You think you can stick your tongue out at me? That's what you get for that," and then she slapped her again. Salomea looked up into the hate-filled eyes. She knew it was pointless to tell her she had not even seen her. The girl walked away, obviously pleased with herself. Salomea ran upstairs crying. What hurt was not so much her cheek, but the injustice of it and her own helplessness.

Instead of just ignoring Salomea's upset, as she so often did, Shayndl said, "Come, Loni, we'll go and talk to the girl's mother."

Salomea was satisfied. Mama would set it right. The girl lived only two houses away. Soon they reached the door and Shayndl rang the bell. A woman opened the door and Shayndl began to explain what happened. "Your daughter slapped mine in the face . . . " But she got no farther.

"What has become of this country, that Germans have to allow Jews to stick their tongues out at them! If we only were rid of you swine . . . "

Salomea lowered her head, trying to concentrate on the pattern of the bristly doormat she was standing on. She could not read and found out only later that such mats usually said "Welcome." She tried in vain to shut her ears to the hatred that hammered down on her. The woman slammed the door in their faces. Sad and helpless, Shayndl looked at Salomea. Neither said a word as they walked back home. A thick cloud of icy hostility enveloped them until they reached the safety of their own apartment.

January 1938. One day Shayndl realized that she did not have enough money for food for the next day. "Malka," she said, "go to Papa and tell him we have no money for food. Tell him to give you something, even if it's only one mark."

Malka took off obediently. Two hours later she came back, very annoyed. "He wants to see Loni. Only if I bring her will he give us something."

Shayndl turned red with anger. "That swine!" she cursed, while helping Salomea into her coat.

Salomea had nothing against the long ride on the S-Bahn. There was so much to see. When she entered the unheated room, she saw her father sitting at the table. Although she had not seen him for almost two years, she recognized him immediately. But she felt nothing as she walked up to him. Her feeling of having been abandoned was deeply buried and could not be dissolved so suddenly. He pulled her toward him, held her between his knees, and stroked her hair. She held still for a few minutes and looked into his sallow face. The room was so cold she could see their breath. Suddenly he put his hand into his pocket, took out a few coins, and gave them to Malka, who impatiently took Salomea by the hand.

"Come on, Loni. We've got to get home!" Reluctantly, he let the child go, and Salomea let herself be pulled away. They turned around once more at the door and looked at the forlorn man with drooping head and shoulders, sitting motionless in his chair. By the time they got home, Salomea had already forgotten her father.

May 1938. Shayndl had agreed to let Avram spend the afternoon with Salomea. Salomea looked forward to this, and she was also excited about her lovely new dress. Shayndl had bought a piece of imitation crepe de chine at a special, low price. It was a light, fluffy fabric in Salomea's favorite color: pink. Shayndl had spent the morning at the sewing machine turning it into a dress.

Salomea walked happily down the street alongside her father. With one hand she held his and with the other she smoothed the creases of her skirt. She looked around to see whether the passersby noticed her dress. When they came to the sandbox on the corner, Avram stopped.

"You can play here," he said, and sat down on the bench. Salomea looked at him, disappointed. She had been looking forward to doing something *with* him. Playing alone in the sandbox she could do any day. But she did not know how to tell him this, and she did as she was told. As she started digging in the sand, he pulled a newspaper from his coat pocket and began to read.

Suddenly she felt a few drops of rain. At first she paid no attention, for Shayndl had always told her, "Ignore it. You're not made of sugar, you won't melt." As the rain got stronger and her dress got wetter, she noticed with horror that the fabric was dissolving where the drops hit it. Soon she would be standing there in her petticoat, in her underwear! She tried to hold back the tears and ran to her Papa to show him the catastrophe.

"Well, then we'd better get back home, hadn't we?" he said, smiling.

"But Papa, I'm in my underwear!" she screeched.

Her panic amused him, and he said, "Look, you're only five. Nobody minds if a little girl like you walks through the street in her underwear."

She found this difficult to believe. She felt so miserable and unhappy as she walked beside him, with her short legs moving as fast as they could. At home, she was the center of both parents' attention for a short while.

The beautiful dress had disintegrated! What a pity! "That's what happens when one buys cheap," said Shayndl in an attempt to comfort her. Salomea thought: Maybe it really is worse to lose the dress than to be seen in the street wearing underwear.

Summer 1938. Salomea became more and more afraid to go out into the street. Since so many Eastern European Jews lived in the Scheunenviertel, it was a favorite marching ground for the SA. When Salomea went home from nursery school with Malka or Shayndl, she heard, and often saw, brown-black columns of marching men, singing loudly. They no longer had faces. They were only moving arms, legs, and mouths, coming toward her like discrete parts of a machine, set in motion for the sole purpose of stamping her, her mother, and her sister into the ground. One line of a song they seemed to sing with particular gusto was: "When Jewish blood spurts from the knife . . . " Then she felt the hand holding hers tighten. "Quick, into the doorway," she would hear Malka say, and they fled into the darkness of an unlit hallway. Only when the sound of the heavy boots on the asphalt had faded did they to go back out into the street and continue on their way home.

September 1938. Salomea had again not seen her father for months. She had become used to the fact that he would appear suddenly and then disappear again, without her knowing why. Now he was there all the time. He lived with them again. True, he slept in the living room and not in the same bed with her mother, as in the old days, but she had him to herself almost all day. Four weeks of unaccustomed warmth and contentment began for Salomea. His face had become thin, and his cheeks were hollower than when she last saw him. He walked with a heavy gait, tired and downcast.

"They wanted a hundred Reichsmarks and an entrance visa, no matter where to," she heard Shayndl tell her neighbors. "Shanghai is the only place Jews are admitted without a sponsor or special conditions. So I got him a visa to go there, and he's leaving soon. I would never take him with me to Australia! The farther away he is from us, the better!" Thus she made it quite clear that she would never forgive the wretch, even if she was helping him now.

During that month, Salomea often sat on Avram's lap. In the first days, Shayndl and Malka sometimes sat opposite them at the living-room table and listened with wide-open, frightened eyes. After his release from the mental institution, Avram had been categorized by the Nazis as a "WS-Jew," meaning work-shy. In June 1938, he was arrested again and taken to the Buchenwald concentration camp. Since he now had a visa and the money had been paid, he was released under the condition that he leave the country within four weeks. He told them, "In the stone quarry, we had to carry big, heavy rocks up a steep slope. The guards had whips with steel tips. Everything had to be done fast, with 'Hep! Hep!'* Those who fell behind got to feel the whips with the steel tips. They were, of course, the weakest and the sickest. And if they couldn't keep up at all, they were simply shot."

Thirty-seven years later, I stood on top of the slope of this stone quarry and remembered my father's words. It was now covered with green grass and looked like a beautiful natural landscape. I watched my ten-year-old son run to the bottom of the ravine. He stooped again and again to dig something out of the ground. "Look, Mutti," he called from afar as he climbed back up again. He held out his hand, and I saw that his palm was full of empty bullet shells.

Avram often sang to Salomea, and she learned the songs quickly. Sometimes they sang together "Sleep then my princess, go to sleep"

---

*"Hep! Hep!" was the cry of the town mobs at the time of the Crusades as they descended on the Jewish quarters to massacre their inhabitants. The origin is debated, but the most widely held view is that it is an acronym for "Hierosulyma est perdita"—Jerusalem is lost. The fact that this was an ancient Jewish city lost to the Moslems didn't keep the Christians from venting their anger against the Jews. The Nazis adopted this tradition, using the cry to make the Jewish prisoners work faster.—Trans.

and "I am a poor vagabond, good night, dear girl, good night."

One day Shayndl came into the room as they were singing this song. "The word is wayfarer, not vagabond!" she said in an irritated voice.

Avram stopped and looked at her sadly. "But I *am* a vagabond, not a wayfarer," he said.

"That's no reason to teach Loni the wrong words!" He gave Salomea a quizzical look and grinned. She nestled against him as if to say: I don't mind learning the wrong words if they are right for you.

"You have to be the hammer, not the anvil, the rider, not the horse," he told her again and again. Salomea did not understand what he meant, but she felt a determination to master everything and a passion for life, whatever it might hold in store.

Avram left at the end of October. Salomea never saw him again.

The poison of my mother's tirades against my father had a profound effect on me that lasted almost a lifetime. When my father wrote to me twenty years later that he wanted to visit me, I replied, "You did not care about me when I was a child and needed you. Now I don't need you anymore either." I was quoting my mother and was convinced that I had written the truth. I needed another twenty-five years before I realized, at the age of fifty, how wrong I had been. Today there is nothing in my life I regret more than this letter.

October 28, 1938. Salomea was woken in the middle of the night by loud knocking on the door. Her mother and sister jumped up and left the room. Salomea listened in the dark, trying to understand what was going on. She heard the gruff voices of two strange men and the intimidated answers of the tenant who slept in the living room, right next to the bedroom. Soon Shayndl and Malka came back to bed, and Salomea fell asleep again.

When Salomea got up the next morning and came into the living room, Shayndl was sitting motionless on a chair in deep thought. She stared at the bales of fabric wrapped in green wax paper and other things belonging to the tenant, who was always dressed in shabby clothes and spoke German with a strong Yiddish accent.

"Where is Herr Grünstein, Mama?" asked Salomea.

"They picked him up during the night," Shayndl replied. "I'm sure he won't come back," she mumbled, more to herself than to her daughter. A few days later, Salomea heard her mother telling her sister that on that night all Jewish men of Polish nationality had been sent back to Poland, but Poland had refused to take them in. Many had wandered up and down along the border, cold and hungry. Some were said to have died.

November 1938, after the pogrom. Salomea entered the building and saw three older children from the neighborhood. They looked at her as if they were planning something. As they did not say anything to her, she passed by them to go upstairs. Now, one after the other ran up behind her and gave her a slap on the back. Salomea felt it, but since it did not hurt, she went on without turning around. She heard the children giggle and run away as if they had done something very bold, for which they could now expect unpleasant consequences. Salomea slowly climbed the stairs and locked herself in the bathroom, the only place where she knew she would not be disturbed. She thought for a long time. Why do they hate us so much? There must be something evil about us, but what? She found no answer, but from then on she could never stop asking questions.

December 3, 1938. "Loni, you don't look Jewish. Go down and get one hundred grams of minced meat and the newspaper. Come, I'll write it down for you. All you have to do is give the butcher this note." Salomea nodded. She had done small errands for her mother before. She knew that today Jews were not allowed to be in the street after twelve o'clock, but if her mother sent her then it must be all right.

She had heard Shayndl warn Malka to come home quickly from school that day. The warning proved unnecessary, since the Jewish girls' school had let the children out early. It had been made known well in advance that December 3 would be "German Solidarity Day." Money was to be collected for the poor. At the street corners men and women reminded the passersby of their duty to give charity with loud cries and the vigorous rattling of collection boxes. Today the Germans wanted to be among themselves; the Jews would not be permitted to spoil the street scene with their presence.

Only after eight o'clock in the evening were they allowed to show themselves again.

Salomea marched off, holding tightly to the money wrapped in the piece of paper. She turned left into Lietzmannstrasse. The butcher and the newspaper shop were only a few doors apart. Darkness set in early on this gray December afternoon. With her package in hand and the folded newspaper under her arm, Salomea walked back home in the dusk. At the corner of Georgenkirchstrasse, she looked up, startled. A boy twice her age and almost twice her size suddenly appeared in front of her. She knew him from the neighborhood. Hands pressed against his hips, a giant looking down on her, he had planted himself in front of her like a wall. He yelled, "What are you doing here? Don't you know Jews are not allowed to show their faces in the street today?" Salomea was seized with terror. The hatred in his eyes and the thundering voice paralyzed her. She could neither answer nor move. She became a disgusting, worthless beetle, good only to be trampled underfoot. She waited. She was sure she would now be killed.

"Get yourself home!" the boy commanded. "If I catch you again, I'll report you to district headquarters. Don't you dare come down again before tomorrow morning!"

His command dissolved her paralysis. She ran as fast as she could, glad that the blow had not been fatal. When she got upstairs, she said nothing about it, and the fear wormed its way deep into her inside.

Was the boy's name Hans? By the time I was fifty-three years old, I had fallen in love with four men named Hans, not to speak of the Fritzes, the Horsts, and the Kurts, and . . . I returned to Berlin from Australia in search of a place where I could feel at home, or so I believed. I did not know that in reality I was seeking acceptance from the "Aryans" to make up for the mistreatment I had received. Whenever an "Aryan" took me into his arms, I was jubilant—I am not a disgusting beetle after all, I am worthy of being loved—until we arranged to meet again. In the first hour of being alone, the hidden fear always came back: He will chase me away. And, from an even deeper level: He will leave me, just as my father did. Then I saw to it that it actually happened. Thus, my conviction was confirmed that I was not worthy of being loved, that the man I love will abuse and abandon me. And this is how I experienced it, again and again and again.

January 1939. Salomea had a constantly recurring nightmare. She and Malka came into the house, and several older children were lying in wait for them in the hallway, ready to beat them up. Malka held tight to her hand and pulled her up the stairs. Salomea tried desperately to keep up with her, but her knees kept giving way, and she just barely managed to get up the stairs, a short step ahead of their tormentors. They reached the apartment and slammed the door shut, despite attempts by their pursuers to prevent it. She always woke from this dream as the wood began to splinter and they were breaking down the door . . .

January 1939. When Malka did the dishes and Salomea dried them, they often sang together. One day they were interrupted by music that came through the kitchen window from the courtyard below. A man was playing a barrel organ, surrounded by a bunch of children. Salomea was allowed to throw him a penny wrapped in a piece of paper. When the man had moved on, Malka sang and Salomea joined in:

We pray and we pray, we have no fear,
One day the light will break through.
We wait and we wait, the time will come,
When Moshiach will set us free.

Malka always said then: "We can wait for him until all eternity. We have to help ourselves!"

February 1939. For some time now, Salomea had been in the habit of crying at bedtime. This had been going on for two weeks; every night the same bawling, and without any reason! The evening always began without anything unusual. When she was told to go to bed, she went into the bedroom, got undressed, and came back into the living room in her nightgown. Then either Mama or Malka took her back to bed. Bedtime stories, fairy tales, or even good-night kisses were unknown to all three of them. Salomea was tucked in with a friendly "sleep tight, sweet dreams." Then Mama or Malka left the room, expecting her to go to sleep.

Once she was alone, all by herself, the events of the past months, weeks, and days began to crowd in on her. As she was falling asleep, she could no longer fight off the images, and she cried.

At first Mama or Malka would come in and ask, "What's the matter?" She could not say, she did not know herself. But their concern calmed her and she fell asleep. After the two weeks, Shayndl lost her patience. Obviously nothing was wrong and still she cried! The crying increasingly got on her nerves.

"I've had enough," she decided one evening. "She just wants attention." Turning to Malka, she added, "If she starts again tomorrow, we'll go for a walk, and again the next evening, until she stops." Malka nodded. Her mother was always right in such matters.

For a while Salomea continued to cry as usual, waiting for either Shayndl or Malka to come. Maybe they didn't hear her, she thought, when nobody came. She now yelled louder, demandingly. When it became clear that nobody would come, the fears overwhelmed her. She was alone and exposed to a merciless world, helpless and vulnerable. Now she called for help as loud as she could. If only somebody, anybody, it didn't have to be Mama or Malka, would come. Nobody came. And Salomea knew why: She didn't deserve to be loved or comforted. Didn't she constantly get on her mother's and sister's nerves with her demands for . . . The child could not name her guilt. Her stomach contracted into a small, tight knot and turned over. Gradually her crying became weaker and, exhausted, she fell asleep. It was the last time Salomea cried before going to sleep. She was cured of *that* habit.

Why, I asked myself thirty years later, do I seek acceptance from precisely those people who have no understanding for me? And why do I soon tire of those who do accept me? Why do I try to square the circle? And why am I often so trusting and naive? In my mid-fifties I began to understand: I am still courting my mother's love, in the vain hope of removing the childhood pain. And because I had pushed away the childhood fears, as an adult I closed my eyes to behavior and actions that should have frightened me. Every little kindness, even if it was only pretense, made me easy prey.

April 30, 1939. Malka wandered through the streets, pulling Salomea behind her. Malka and Shayndl had separated to get the last stamps and papers for leaving Germany, for the transit through

Italy and entering Australia. The train ride to Genoa and the ship's passage to Melbourne had been booked, and the Jewish community had paid the fare.

It was a quarter to one. The Italian embassy would close in fifteen minutes. They had missed each other at the place where they had agreed to meet. Now the fourteen-year-old was desperately looking around for her mother. They were to depart the next day. If she did not find her mother now, they would not get the transit visa in time. Would they then ever be able to get away from here? From the distance she suddenly heard the familiar voice call her name. Thank God! Now the three of them rushed to the embassy. Five to one! Shayndl rang the bell. A grumbling doorkeeper opened the door and called the official. He asked them in and told them to sit down. Soon he came back with the completed passports. He bade them a friendly farewell, giving all three a handshake: "The very best of luck to you on your long journey."

Relieved and happy, they left the building. Salomea again trotted between them. "The policeman at the station was also quite nice," Shayndl said. "They're not all beasts. He actually seemed to feel sorry."

That was a small consolation on the eve of the great involuntary adventure.

❖

Epilogue

I went to school in Australia and grew up there. Since I was unhappy with my family—I hated my mother without admitting it even to myself—I looked for a substitute family and found it in the Communist Party. In time, my relationship with the party became more important to me than my family, friends, or even lovers. For the party would never abandon or hurt me as they could.

And yet, I felt like a stranger in Australia. In my search for a place where I could feel at home, I moved to the German Democratic Republic. I tried to be a German communist, became a mother, and experienced the routine of everyday life. In the course of twenty years, during which I tried in vain to gain a political voice, I finally realized: I am living in a banal police state, such as they have existed throughout the ages, in many ways worse than the capitalism I had left behind. I was deeply shaken when I recognized myself in Hannah Arendt's description of the totally loyal comrade: "Such loyalty can be expected only from the completely isolated human being who, without any other social ties to family, friends, comrades, or even mere acquaintances, derives his sense of having a place in the world only from his belonging to a movement, his membership in the party."* After a complete nervous breakdown and the psychotherapy that followed, I summed up my experience of fifty-five years in 1986 on Yom Kippur, the Jewish holy day of atonement:

> Fifty years of fear unnoticed,
> Fifty years of tears uncried.
> Mama, why don't you see me crying?
> Mama, why don't you listen to me?
> Mama, why doesn't Papa come back?
> Mama, I'm cold. Why don't you comfort me?

*Hannah Arendt, *The Origins of Totalitarianism* (New York: Harcourt Brace Jovanovich, 1973), 323–24.

Fifty years of fear unnoticed,
Fifty years of tears uncried.
Judah verrecke! Don't buy from Jews!
You dirty Jew, poke your tongue out at me?
She's Jewish, slap her in the face!
Called the blond, blue-eyed Aryans.

Mama, why do they hate us so?
Mama, I'm cold. Why don't you comfort me?
Because I'm bad, I get no comfort,
Because Jews are evil, the Aryans hate us.
Fifty years of fear unnoticed.
Fifty years of tears uncried.

Forty years of self-hatred and flight from the monster: Me.
Forty years of longing for the father lost.
Forty years of longing for the repentant Aryan.
Forty years of devoted love—for the Party!
Forty years of comfort sought—in the Party!
Forty years of self-denial—for the Party!
Forty years of fear unnoticed in others!
Forty years of unnoticed lies!

Forty years of a life gone wrong.

Mama! I'm cold! Why didn't you comfort me?

✻

Glossary

Adar	Sixth month of the Jewish calendar (corresponding to February/March).
hametz	Not kosher for Passover.
milchig and fleishig	Referring to milk and meat products, which are not allowed to be mixed according to Jewish dietary laws.
Moshiach	Yiddish for Messiah.
Poale Zion	"Workers of Zion"; Jewish workers' movement within the Zionist movement; originated in Russia at the beginning of the century.
S-Bahn	Berlin elevated train.
schmonzes	Colloquial: exaggerations, fancies.
stibl	A small prayer and study room.
treife	Not pure; opposite of kosher.
Wschod	A Lemberg weekly Polish newspaper with a Zionist orientation.
yeckes, yeckishe	Derogatory description of German Jews because they wore jackets (*yeckes*).

❖

Afterword

WOLFGANG BENZ

The historian, whose task it is to place the story of Shayndl and Salomea within a historical context of dates and facts, must also acknowledge that this story of an Eastern European Jewish family bears the mark of the miraculous. The probability that a family like the Genins would escape from Hitler's Germany was small, considering the bureaucratic hurdles standing in the way of emigration from Germany as well as immigration to one of the few countries willing to take in the exiles. Many German Jews faltered in their attempt to emigrate because of lack of affidavits, failure to obtain visas (or if visas were obtained, they often turned out to be invalid), the inability to pay for passage, political restrictions, and the callousness of (often anti-Semitic) consular officials.

For a poor family of Eastern European Jews lacking German passports—even more for someone like Avram, who had strayed into the realm of the social misfit—the odds were particularly unfavorable. But Shayndl's and her daughters' poverty was also their saving grace. Because of it, the Jewish community of Berlin took them under its wing and bore their travel expenses. It was invaluable in those days to have a relative in the United States, Canada, or Australia, like Shayndl's brother Bezalel in Melbourne, who signed an affidavit first for Rebecca and then for Shayndl, Malka, and Salomea. Just as important was a timely decision to leave Germany. For the tens of thousands of Jews who began to make plans for emigration only after Kristallnacht, on November 9, 1938, the race with time was often lost. By the fall of 1939, the outbreak of the war largely blocked the way, foreign consulates and embassies closed down, and visa applications remained unprocessed. Even for those many tens of thousands who had sought refuge in time in the Netherlands, France, Czechoslovakia, and Italy, exile became a trap when German troops conquered the guest countries and forced their governments to hand over the Jews, virtually ensuring their death.

On May 4, 1939, Shayndl, Malka, and Salomea take the train
from Berlin to Genoa. Two days later they set sail for Melbourne on
the Italian steamer *Esquilino*. They arrive four weeks later in their
new country. Rebecca, Shayndl's eldest daughter, who had already
been in the country for eighteen months and had a job as a cashier
at a butcher shop, had rented an apartment, bought furniture on
credit, and paid the first installment. Shayndl is appalled by the
whole arrangement and immediately sets out to look for something
better. She finds a house at the low rent of only thirty-two shillings
a week. When the war breaks out, all rents are frozen, a godsend for
Shayndl. When the owners put the house up for sale after the war,
she is able to acquire it for a reasonable price.

This does not mean that she is suddenly well-to-do in this foreign country. During her first five or six years there, Shayndl makes
a living as a washerwoman, keeping the clothes of single, male emigrants in order. Later she works for dry goods stores and organizes
cutting and sewing jobs for women working at home. Malka is
apprenticed to a glovemaker, and Salomea, almost seven, must
attend school virtually straight off the boat. It had made no sense
for her to start school in Berlin so shortly before their emigration.
The shock of Australia, therefore, is magnified for her. Salomea
always runs away because she does not understand anything,
because she is scared of the strange children, because her only English at beginning is "a pot of tea, a pot of coffee, a pot of honey."
Only when another German-speaking emigrant child befriends her
is she able—within three months—to learn English. She speaks the
language without a trace of a foreign accent.

Later, because she often seems depressed, Malka takes the
twelve-year-old Salomea to meetings of the communist youth association, where she finds a home, security, and a purpose. In 1948,
after eight years of schooling (the customary education for young
girls in Australia), Salomea takes a secretarial course, and in 1949
she takes an office job with a trade union. Soon she advances to
youth secretary of the Jewish Council to Combat Fascism and Anti-
Semitism. When the fervent communist hears that the Communist
Youth World Festival of 1951 will take place in East Berlin, she
moves heaven and earth to become part of the Australian delega-
tion. She pays for her travel expenses with her savings, finds the

German Democratic Republic fascinating, and is convinced that she would find there a new type of human being, a new society, and a just world. Salomea plans to stay in the GDR for six months to see whether the reality would live up to her fantasy. She seeks in East Germany a political and geographic home, which she had been unable to find in Australia.

But the German Democratic Republic is not interested in new citizens. The festival would last two weeks. She would be able to stay one week longer to tour the country. Salomea receives no response to her application for a residence permit. Frustrated, she returns to Australia. She sends two vain requests to Erich Honecker, then the functionary in charge of youth affairs, for permission to immigrate. Yet undaunted and persistent, she continues to pursue her goal. After three years, during which she saves every penny she can with iron determination, she returns to Europe in 1954. She lives in West Berlin, then for a longer time in England, and then again in West Berlin. At long last, in May 1963, she gains admission to the GDR.

Her hopes, of course, are not fulfilled. The story of her life in the German Democratic Republic—the story of her illusions, reality, and identity—she has described elsewhere.

Something remains to be said about the fate of Shayndl and Avram. "In spite of herself on her own feet"—this is how Salomea describes her mother's life in Australia—Shayndl becomes involved with a man who will not marry her even though she lives with him for seven years. To prove to herself and to the world that she is still desirable, she marries someone else. The marriage lasts exactly six months. In 1956, Shayndl moves to Israel for the first time and lives there almost three years. Then follows a terrible year for mother and daughter when Shayndl lives with Salomea in Berlin. In 1959, she returns to Melbourne and her older daughters.

At the age of eighty-two, over Malka's virulent objections, the restless woman sells her house in Melbourne—the one she had rented in 1939 and bought in 1948—in order to settle finally in Israel. She is already gravely ill when she arrives there. After a fall, she is forced to return to Australia for long-term hospital treatment. A little more than two years later, Shayndl Genin, age eighty-five, dies of a heart attack in the street in Melbourne.

Avram, Shayndl's divorced husband and Salomea's father, is able to leave Berlin in time. He spends the war years in Shanghai. Then, after a brief stay in a camp in West Germany, he emigrates to the United States in 1949. He tries once again to carve out a livelihood for himself, this time with a dry cleaning operation, but in vain. In the end, he is forced to live on welfare. He dies in Washington, D.C., in 1972.

❀

Jewish Lives